The
Numinous Site

The Numinous Site

The Poetry
of Luis Palés Matos

Julio Marzán

Madison • Teaneck
Fairleigh Dickinson University Press
London: Associated University Presses

Associated University Presses
440 Forsgate Drive
Cranbury, NJ 08512

Associated University Presses
25 Sicilian Avenue
London WC1A 2QH, England

Associated University Presses
P.O. Box 338, Port Credit
Mississauga, Ontario
Canada L5G 4L8

The paper used in this publication meets the requirements
of the American National Standard for Permanence of Paper
for Printed Library Materials Z39.48-1984.

Library of Congress Cataloging-in-Publication Data

Marzán, Julio, 1946–
    The numinous site : the poetry of Luis Palés Matos / Julio Marzán.
        p.   cm.
    Includes bibliographical references and index.
    ISBN 0-8386-3581-4 (alk. paper)
    1. Palés Matos, Luis—Criticism and interpretation.   I. Title.
PQ7439.P24Z76   1995
861—dc20   94-47234
                                                                        CIP

PRINTED IN THE UNITED STATES OF AMERICA

Contents

The
Numinous Site

1

Poetry and Antipoetry:
From *Canciones* to *Tuntún*

Starting in 1925, a number of poets mainly from the Caribbean but not exclusively, published what is broadly called *poesía negra*. Different from African American poetry in English, *poesía negra* was called black even when the poet wasn't, but the same bias prevails among the critics, who stereotype it as a sort of quasi-oral style, requiring an anthropological and social investigation, a justification for treating it as marginal to the evolving poetics of implicitly white, written poetry. This pattern holds true even among supportive critics, those specializing in traditionally over-looked literatures. Those critics customarily study *poesía negra*[1] in a "Nativist," ethnological, or political framework that deprives *poesía negra* of strictly literary significance, effectively segregating that poetry from any conversation on its contribution to contemporary Latin American poetics. Owing to this convention, *poesía negra* has been woefully misrepresented as has been the genealogy of contemporary Latin American poetry. Thus readers and critics have failed to appreciate that with *poesía negra*, notably in the work of its most prominent figures, Luis Palés Matos and Nicolás Guillén, Latin American poetry took its first step toward the ironic, conversational, comic, mordant, quotidian, and unpoetic consciousness that decades later encompassed what the Uruguayan Mario Benedetti termed "poesía comunicante" and the Chilean Nicanor Parra called "antipoetry."

In *The Antipoetry of Nicanor Parra*, Edith Grossman details three objectives of "the theoretical course" that Parra "set for himself after the publication of his *Cancionero sin Nombre*."[2] The first objective was to free poetry from the domination of the metaphor, which he terms "the abuse of earlier poetic language" (Grossman, 8). His antipoetry, understood as a liberation from what he termed as "abusive" style, would rather avoid such "poetic" language in favor of direct communication with the reader. Second,

9

antipoetry should "depend on the commonplace in all its ramifications, that it decisively reject the rarefied and the exotic, both thematically and linguistically" (Grossman, 8). By this, Grossman elucidates, Parra meant that "the language of literature must be no different from the language of the collectivity . . . language reflects the life of the people. . . ."[3] Third, Parra has reaffirmed that his writing was leading directly to a "purely national expression (Skármeta, 39)" (Grossman, 9) because the poet cannot remove himself from the community, the tribe. Thus the poet "should use colloquialisms peculiar to his own country, even if readers from other areas find them difficult to understand."[4]

These objectives, of course, are ideals. Starting with its title, *Canciones Rusas* contain a good number of exoticisms (from a Chilean viewpoint, of course). And as his own title *Poemas y Antipoemas* (1954) well illustrates, Parra himself was aware that antipoets are only at best half-time antipoets. Consequently, while he aspired to liberate the poem entirely from the domination of the metaphor, in practice he often simply turned the speaking persona into a neo-romantic persona-metaphor, as in "El Soliloquo del Individuo" or "El Peregrino," who ultimately resorts to the claim of being "Un árbol que pide a gritos se le cubra de hojas," or the "Autorretrato" in the tradition of Robert Browning. These are a form of Chilean blues. Similarly, the metaphor is still central in "La Montaña Rusa," whose titular metaphor describes his new poetry. A similar contradiction operates in the poem whose title asks "¿Qué Es la Antipoesía?" and which subsequently responds with a catalogue of metaphors.

As Benedetti has noted, Parra is a hybrid among several other makers of new poetry. What Parra did, Benedetti observes, was to take on the voice of the existentialist tragedian in Neruda's *Residencias* and make it say wholly different and novel things:

> . . . even though Parra occasionally assumes an anti-Neruda posture, at bottom he is the one who receives from the poet of the *Residencias* the baton of the word, and instead of fracturing or repudiating it, makes it say something else, original and fertile before passing it on to Enrique Lihn, who also rather than break it down enriches it. And of course one can establish other paths and other almost parallel lineages, . . .[5]

In other words, Latin American poetry has evolved without a break from or a repudiation of its antecedents. Antipoetry, as José Ibáñez Langlois affirms in his introduction to the Spanish edition of Parra's selected poems, *Antipoemas*, was simply a stage in the continuous enrichment of a poetic lineage; it was just another category of poetry:

> The antipoem isn't, of course, anything other than a poem: we must eliminate any mythology surrounding it. Parra himself says of it that "after all, it is no other thing than the traditional poem enriched with the juices of surrealism—creole surrealism or whatever you want to call it—" . . .The question, then, is one of cleansing European surrealism of its artifice, of its useless obscurity, its decadent uprooting of life, by means of a local answer—and only for that very reason a universal one—bound to an everyday language and a real experience of man *in situ*. . . ."[6]

Being poetry, the antipoem has a long history and the epithet "antipoetry" is generally applicable to poetry in a tradition of rebellion. Thus, the term "antipoetry" can also apply to "all poetic responses against exhaustion, verbal routine, prefabricated emotions, forms that are derivative and now dead to the language and lived experience."[7] Ibáñez sees Parra's style as hinging on two key devices, irony and personae. These helped Parra take antipoetry to conversational language and even farther from traditional poetic forms; these have been Parra's two chief weapons against the lyric voice and the preeminence of the first person.

But while irony and personae may have been revolutionary in the standard literary context, there were technical elements that had already characterized important Latin American poetry in a literary lineage that the criticism simply overlooked, namely in *poesía negra*. In the late 1930's, Parra was theorizing about a poetry with ingredients that had already been used to the same rebellious effects in Latin America for almost a decade, anthologized (by de Onís in a 1934 anthology that included "Canción Festiva"), and popularized in night club performances. By every standard, including Parra's three objectives, Guillén's "Tú No Sabe Inglé," a satire on cultural imperialism, is also the consummate antipoem:

> TU NO SABE INGLE
> Con tanto inglé que tú sabía,
> Vito Manuel,
> con tanto inglé, no sabe ahora
> decir: ye.
>
> La mericana te buca,
> y tú le tiene que huir:
> tu inglé era detrai guan,
> detrai guan y guan tu tri . . .

Vito Manuel, tú no sabe inglé,
tú no sabe inglé,
tú no sabe inglé.

No te namore más nunca,
Vito Manué,
si no sabe inglé,
si no sabe inglé.

[All that English you 'pose to know,
Vito Manuel,
All that English, now you can't
even say: yes.

The *americana* lady chases you,
and you gotta run:
your English just for *estrike guan*,
estrike guan, and *guan, two, tree.*

Vito Manuel, you can't talk English,
you can't talk English,
you can't talk English.

Don't you ever fall in love,
Vito Manué,
if you can't talk English,
if you can't talk English.][8]

In this poem, the traditional lyric's metaphor is non-existent and irony and persona are the chief poetic devices.

"Tú No Sabe Inglé" was originally published in Guillén's first book *Motivos de Son*, which appeared in 1930. That was seven years before the publication of Luis Palés Matos's *Tuntún de Pasa y Grifería: Poesía Afro-Antillana*, but four years after the publication of Palés's first *poema negro* in 1925 (which according to both Margot Arce de Vázquez and Federico de Onís was a poem titled "Africa," which after revisions later appeared in *Tuntún* under the title "Pueblo Negro"), and three years after the 1927 publication of José Robles Pazo's critical article in Madrid in *La Gaceta Literaria*, introducing Palés's *poesía negra* to the Spanish-speaking literary world. The publication of those first poems and their critical recognition as evidenced by that article marked the start of a school that critics, such as Mónica Mansour, today look back and call a "movimiento" that Palés is credited with having initiated:

The *poesía negrista* as a literary movement was begun around 1926 by the Puerto Rican Luis Palés Matos and was enriched by the major contributions of Nicolás Guillén, Emilio Ballagas, Regino Pedroso, Manuel del Cabral and their emulators.[9]

The milestone 1927 selection of Palés's work published in Madrid consisted of "Candombe," "Kalahari" and, key here, "Canción Festiva para Ser Llorada" ["Festive Song to Be Wept"], a poem that was the forerunner of later poets' subsequent poetry of personae and irony. In that poem, for example, we hear the voice of Palés's *habanero*, easily a cousin of Guillén's later "Vito Manué." Without the phonetic recreation in Guillén's poem, this *habanero* warns a woman, Cubanly referred to as "niña," to beware of the "ñáñigo," a member of secret society of black Cubans:

> Mira que te coge el ñáñigo,
> niña, no salgas de casa.
> Mira que te coge el ñáñigo
> del juegito de la Habana.
> Con tu carne hará gandinga,
> con tu seso mermelada;
> ñáñigo carabalí
> de la manigua cubana.

> [Out there's the *ñáñigo*,
> girl, don't leave the house.
> Out there's the *ñáñigo*
> from the Havana sect.
> With your flesh he'll make a stew,
> with your brains a marmelade,
> that Carabar-blooded *ñáñigo*
> from the Cuban bush.][10]

Despite the warning, the "niña," another kin to Vito Manuel, will go out in her "saya" (instead of the Puerto Rican "falda") to dance in the "titiringó":

> Me voy al titiringó
> de la calle de la prángana,
> ya verás el huele-huele
> que enciendo tras de mi saya,
> cuando resude canela
> sobra la rumba de llamas;
> que a mí no me arredra el ñáñigo
> del jueguito de la Habana.

[I'm going to the blow out
on the uproar street,
soon you'll smell the smoke
I ignite under my skirt,
when my cinnamon sweats
over the rumba of flames;
'cause the Havana sect *ñáñigo*,
he don't frighten me.]

As should be apparent from the above citations, humor is a hallmark of Palés's Afro-Antillean poems, and it appears in two key elements, irony and punning. Ironic humor, for example, underlies "Ñáñigo al Cielo," which depicts the ascendence of a black Cuban to a white Western heaven, which has decorated itself for the "milagroso ascenso":

El ñáñigo sube al cielo.
El cielo se ha decorado
de melón y calabaza
por la entrada del ñáñigo.

[The *ñáñigo* climbs to heaven.
Heaven has been decked out
with melons and pumpkins
for the *ñáñigo*'s entrance.]

In the white man's heaven as in a white man's world, the black is treated as an exotic, to be studied and gawked at:

En loa del alma nueva
que el Empíreo ha conquistado,
ondula el cielo en escuadras
de doctores y de santos.
Con arrobos maternales,
a que contemplen el ñáñigo
las castas once mil vírgenes
traen a los niños nonatos.

[In honor of the new soul
the Empyrean has won,
squadrons of doctors of the church and saints
fly in waves across the skies.
Maternally ecstatic,
the chaste eleven thousand virgins
bring their unborn children
so they may see the *ñáñigo*.]

Another of Palés's other major weapons against the serious and expected was the pun, a staple of *conceptismos* from the baroque, clearly a style by which he was influenced. But in punning, Palés was being very much a nativist. The Caribbean mind revels in word play, especially sexually charged ambiguity. We hear it in conversation. We hear it in the lyrics of popular songs such as Dominican *merengues* and Puerto Rican *guarachas* and *plenas*. Similarly, the writings of Guillermo Cabrera Infante, José Lezama Lima, Luis Rafael Sánchez and, most recently, Ana Lydia Vega are distinctly characterized by that regional penchant for burlesque-level word-play. The chronic punning and language tricks in those writers express a broader regional sense of language humor that, in the tradition of *poesía negra*, those writers continue to infuse into Latin American literature. While a case may be made that the Caribbean penchant is a monument to the enduring influence of the colonial baroque period on the Caribbean, that period has ended and the penchant remains to characterize the regional culture. Moreover, this overlooks the widely established African traditions of language humor, evident in music. Thus, as will be shown in greater depth later, the ludic Palés is also a helpless, Caribbean punster.

Unfortunately, because Guillén's work is more readily identifiable as social rebellion, since the sixties the Cuban poet has overshadowed Luis Palés Matos with his misunderstood, brainy, baroque style. As Guillén became symbol and patriarch of the Cuban postrevolutionary poets, the Revolution itself, having become a world generation's icon of anti-bourgeois, anti-Westernist society, even in Puerto Rico leftist poets rejected Palés Matos as a racist who ridiculed and exploited African culture. In contrast, Guillén, a true black voice and a Marxist, appeared to speak more directly to the condition of the Third World. The trouble with this analysis is that it pits Palés against Guillén when Palés preceded Guillén, performed the literary moves that set the stage for Guillén to surface, and was a Latin American original: a white man who, in the 1920's, dared to reflect publicly on his culture's African roots.

Additionally, in publicizing his radical vision, Palés contributed to Latin American poetry a stylistic *mulatez* that, consistent with his Afro-Antillean theme, combined "white" poetic structures with "black" unconventional humor, social satire, drumbeat rhythms, and most important, an unprestigious, African-derived vocabulary. That enriched Spanish, according to Palés, characterized his society, even its literate speech, giving the island a unique, Caribbean identity. This is the language his prefatory poem "Preludio en Boricua" ("Prelude in Boricua") proclaims and celebrates as the language of his book of Afro-Antillean poems. "Boricua" here refers to the language of "boricuas," or Puerto Rican Spanish. Not a dialect, or a radical departure from standard Spanish grammar, "boricua" is the national flavor or idiom, characterized by a wealth of non-standard or regional words, phrases and idiomatic expressions whose origin is African. Language as the prime motif in Palés's *poesía afro-antillana* is also, if more subtly, evident in the final title of the book itself, *Tuntún de pasa y Grifería* (*Tomtom of Kinky Hair and Black Things*). The rhythmic title is popular speech. Besides the obvious onomatopoetic highlighting of the dominant rhythm in these poems, the title also metaphorically compares the poems to a communication by drumbeat: the book is a *tuntún*.

Other revealing concepts operate in that title. "Pasa," denoting kinky hair, a definitive sign of blackness in Puerto Rican society, echoes the verb form "pasa" as in "passing"; "grifería," derived from "grifo," another reference to tight curly hair, is a racial epithet with additional nuances in Puerto Rico. Originally, a "grifo" was a cross between a mulatto and a black, or a quadroon. Rubén del Rosario tells us simply that a "grifo" is a white person with African physical traits.[11] But the term also connotes a social and psychological stereotype. In his essay *Insularismo*, albeit tinged with his characteristic racism, Antonio S. Pedreira defines this stereotype:

> Decidedly and vehemently, the *grifo* struggles from the bottom of his conscience for a full recognition of his faculties and for egalitarian treatment that would assure him his piece of opportunity in life.[12]

"Grifería," then, also addresses features and a character type, signifying to behave like an African and looking for equal recognition, a description that can carry over to colonized whites as well. So while the idea of *negro* or negritude is evoked by the titular words, the title itself addresses black attitudes and physical or psychological features that, strictly speaking, have nothing to do with color of skin, which was Palés's point: his *poesía* was what it purported to be, not *negra* but *afroantillana*.

As Palés explained, his objective was to define, through the medium of language, the culture shared by the Caribbean islands, notably the Spanish-speaking islands that share the same two roots:

In the first place, I've never spoken of a black, white or mulatto poetry; I've only spoken of an Antillean poetry that, culturally-speaking,
reflects our collective reality. I sustain that the Antilles—Cuba, Santo
Domingo, Puerto Rico—have developed a homogeneous spiritual
type and are therefore psychologically tuned in one common direction. And I further sustain that this spiritual homogeneity is absolutely different from the common masses of Hispanic peoples and
that in [our homogeneity] the negroide factor intermixed in the Antillean psyche has served as a separator, or in chemical terms, as a
precipitative agent. (Palés, 219)

It was the color consciousness in the Spanish-speaking world
that caused his poems to take on a life of their own according to
the public's response to things having to do with *negros*. Misread
with this mindset, the Afro-Antillean poems found a broad audience, even to the sound of drums in Latin America's night clubs,
as well as among the literati, among whom the black arts were
in vogue. But while this reception broadened Palés's reputation,
it also censored out the revolutionary and serious purpose of
these poems by reaffirming the convention that Caribbean social
reality provides material inherently useful in entertainments but
of marginal literary value. That preconception surfaces in another
criticism launched at Palés: the folly of his attempt to write sophisticated literature by veering from the standard Spanish and
writing with local bastardizations of it. Palés addressed the issue
squarely in "Hacia una Poesía Afroantillana" ("Toward an Afro-
Antillean Poetry"). Citing the Bible, Cervantes, Dante, and Ru-
bens, he noted that all great works of art began with popular
elements:

In any corner of the planet where there are men, that is, rhythm of
life, plays of passions, shuffling of interests in motion, a masterpiece
can appear. The important thing is that the artist's creative genius
focus on the environment surrounding those cardinal accents that
touch upon the very essence of humanity. (Palés, 223)

Palés's interest in capturing the essence of his environment was
partly a result of an early influence from Walt Whitman. In a 1927
interview, he explained how, from Whitman, he learned to write
into his own poems those elements that literature had left out
because they were considered unpoetic:

Walt Whitman was the first who went against the dying ideology of
symbolism, raising his weighty and orquestral massiveness in the

praise of everything that previous poets would have thought sacrili-
gious: the machine, the factory, tumultuous and laboring human be-
ings; all themes concordant with the world's industrial and scientific
development.[13]

Compare Palés's comments with Parra's description of what he
saw valuable in Whitman, in a quotation from an interview:

It's an open poetry, there is no strict subject matter or conventional
poetic language. The poems are like poetic studies, not little lyrical
verses. Description is very important to Whitman's poetry; there are
even narratives, brief stories interpolated throughout his *Leaves of
Grass* . . . the enormous quantity of materials and the freedom with
which he works them, . . . I think these were the lines of development that touched me deeply, ...[14]

Although Palés was not, as Parra assumed the reputation of
being, a theorizer about poetry, on varying interpretative levels
a good number of Palés's poems are about the nature of poetry.
The Filí-Melé cycle, resonant with Heideggerian ideas, philosophically reflects on poetry as the experiencing of Being. The
book, *Tuntún de Pasa y Grifería*, by fusing poetic and antipoetic
elements, is a statement on poetry. We can extrapolate his poetics
from poems such as "Preludio en Boricua," "Canción Festiva para
Ser Llorada," "Plena del Menéalo" ("Shake It *Plena*"). In "El
Menú," he turns his poetics into a conceit, speaking as the host
of a restaurant. His poetry-restaurant offers food that is cooked
without the tricks of an "especiosa culinaria," the modifier "especiosa" evoking both spicy and specious:

> Mi estorán abierto en el camino
> para ti, trashumante peregrino.
> Comida limpia y varia
> sin truco de especiosa culinaria.
>
> [My restaurant open on the road
> for you, pasture-seeking pilgrim.
> Clean and varied food,
> artful not in specious cookery.]

His use of the popular *anglicismo* "restorán," aside from celebrating Caribbean spoken language, satirically puns with
"restos," or waste, which is how the Caribbean culture is popularly perceived from a Euro-centered point of reference. Also note
the ironic use of "trashumante," a modifier that refers to herded

animals driven to distant pastures but whose sound evokes the travelling of humans.

The host then offers dishes—concocted from images taken from the Caribbean landscape, geography, and foods—appealing to a range of tastes. He even informs the "pilgrim" of available Frenchified dishes like those whipped up by the chef Rubén Darío, dishes that are obviously not Palés's favorite, but that the house can also offer:

> Tengo, para los gusto ultrafinos,
> platos que son la gloria de la mesa . . .
> aquí están unos pinos,
> pinos a la francesa
> en verleniana salsa de crepúsculo.
> (El chef Rubén, cuyos soberios flanes
> delicia son de líricos gurmanes,
> les dedicó un opúsculo).

> [I have, for ultrafine tastes,
> dishes that crown any table . . .
> here a serving of pines,
> pines *Francaise*
> in Verlanian twilight sauce.
> (Chef Rubén, whose tame custards
> enthrall poetry's gourmands,
> honored them with an opuscule).]

Satirical puns abound in this stanza. The modifier "ultrafinos" suggests homosexual. The "pinos" ("pines"), with their etymological kinship to penis, evoke the pine's erectness (as in "empinar," to stand straight up). Besides being cooked in a French manner, the "pinos" are also served "a la francesa," whose idiomatic meaning is brusquely, without saying a word (usually upon leaving). These are "pinos" served brusquely in a sauce of "crepúsculo," which consists of the *crepus*, curly, and the obvious *culo*. Similarly, *opús-culo* can be read as one word or two. All this satire is addressed not only to the French and regrettably, homosexuals, but as well to the less discriminating "gurmanes" of the poem. The host then lists what foods he would rather offer:

> Si a lo francés, prefieres lo criollo,
> y tu apetito, con loable intento,
> pírrase por ajiaco y ajopollo
> y sopón de embrujado condimento,
> toma este calalú maravilloso

> con que la noche tropical aduna
> su maíz estrellado y luminoso,
> y el diente de ajo de su media luna
> en divino potaje sustancioso.
>
> [If to French, you prefer creole
> and your appetite, with commendable designs,
> craves hot sauce, seasoned chicken,
> and a soup of bewitched condiments,
> taste this enchanting calalú,
> in which the tropic night combines
> its shining, star-like grains of corn
> and its garlic-clove half moon
> in a hearty celestial pottage.]

The poem celebrates the poetic possibilities of this Caribbean treasure of images from which the host is able to whip up unheard of creations:

> Aquí te va una muestra:
> palmeras al ciclón de las Antillas,
> cañaveral horneado a fuego lento,
> soufflé de plantanales sobre el viento,
> piñón de flamboyanes en su tinta, . . .
>
> [Here is a sample:
> palm trees tossed in Antillean cyclone,
> slow-flame broiled sugar cane
> sufflé of windblown plantain groves,
> pie of flamboyants in their ink, . . .]

As Palés, the restauranteur, points out in offering "pinos a la francesa," part of his training was *modernista*, and he was aware that its influence still resided in his new poetics.

What is being argued here is that Palés's *poesía afroantillana* popularized the "dark" forces (African roots, the literary legitimacy of unprestigious speech) that were the white, *criollo* society's antimatter, an antipoetic consciousness that, subsequently complemented and refined by Guillén, liberated the later *conversante* poetry. Williams Carlos Williams, who traveled to Puerto Rico in 1941, met Palés Matos and later read *Tuntún de Pasa y Grifería*, readily saw this affinity between himself and this poet from his mother's homeland. Williams published "Prelude in Boricua," his translation of "Preludio en Boricua." While Palés's near-Gongorine style and Williams's apparent free-flowing verse[15] may seem incompatible, Williams immediately grasped that Palés had written a poetry that uses local talk and humor with utmost seriousness. Furthermore, in one of several encoded expressions of poetic kinship and tribute, for the final "scheme" for *Paterson* Williams borrowed Palés' model of invoking the inspiriting essence of the Caribbean by addressing it as a love object in "Mulata-Antilla" ("Mulatto Woman-Island"). Williams, who guarded his sources, didn't state this outright, but the evidence is in the chronology when Williams started writing *Paterson* and in the poem itself. Book One contains a subtle homage to Palés in the form of a poem on an African king and his wives, a poem with rather transparent borrowings from "Elegía del Duque de la Mermelada" ("Elegy of the Duke of Marmelade") and "Majestad Negra" ("Majestad Negra"). The point to underscore is that, as a poet accused of being an antipoet, who furthermore campaigned on behalf of a truly American-spirited poetry that broke with Europe by elevating an American idiom, Williams appreciated that Palés Matos was certainly qualified to play in his band.

Nicanor Parra too also acknowledged, in a 1973 New York University graduate seminar[16] on the origins of his antipoetry, that as a young poet he had read *Tuntún* and was impressed by its sense of humor and certain antipoetic imagery. Parra then read from a personal copy of what seemed like a very early edition of *Tuntún de Pasa y Grifería*. He singled out "Elegía del Duque de la Mermelada," noting the antipoetic quality of images such as "y sus quinces mujeres olorosas a selva y a fango" ["and his fifteen wives smelling of mud and the jungle"]. Except for that occasion, however, Parra has not mentioned Palés in any other discussion on the origins of his antipoetry. Given the convention that discourages comparing the aesthetics of "white" and "black" poetry, Parra's omission is understandable. So, too, one understands why Benedetti and Grossman were blindsided from seeing a precedent for today's *poesía comunicante* or *antipoesía* in *poesía negra* or *poesía afroantillana*.

But the fact remains that in virtually every Western art form in this century the search for an antiform has led to a gravitation to the "dark" forces. Unfortunately, we come to this admission reluctantly, in keeping with the long denial of the racial impurity of Western civilization. Classical scholarship is only now debating how much the West has distorted its history to camouflage the degree to which it is indebted to Africa by way of Egypt, Greece and Rome. Owing to this pattern, throughout the Americas the idea of *negro*, and by extension the niggerized *indio*, has performed the role of antimatter to Euro-centered myths of national cultures. In the fifties, the U.S. Anglo who chose to defy middle class life with an alternate, forbidden lifestyle became a Beatnik, whom Norman Mailer termed "The White Negro." As part of their rebellion, they chose jazz over classical or mainstream popular music. Similarly, when white teenagers of the fifties rebelled against Eisenhower's America they gravitated to the nascent dances and records of rock and roll, which were originally forbidden over the air waves for being "nigger music." In the following decade, the counterculture was synonymous with the Civil Rights movement.

We are dealing with a dynamic: *poesía negra* must be understood in a broader context of the century, playing its part in literature as jazz had patently done in dance and music—and literature. In that dynamic, spontaneous jazz poems were also an antimatter that removed the white mask from an inherently mixed culture. Similarly, in an island that until the late fifties excluded from public air waves the musical legacy from Africa— *plena, guaracha—poesía afroantillana* was to Palés a countercultural expression, an antipoetry. Likewise, the *poetas comunicantes*, whose key figures identified with the political left and exhibited a social consciousness that went beyond their generation's already fashionable dabbling in negritude, certainly read Guillén and Palés in their youth and were directly, even if not wittingly, informed by the antecedent of *poesía negra*. Before the *poetas comunicantes* received the influence of Whitman, surrealism and dadaism, Afro-Antillean poetry and all the other *poesía negra* had tasted that liberation. By setting Luis Palés Matos's work—and subsequent *poesía negra* — in the proper literary context, we begin to see that in Latin America the shift to a combination of spoken language, irony, humor, satire, and social consciousness was first made in the Caribbean.

Palés's awareness of the border between those two aesthetics was rooted in his cultural history, in the tension between the romanticized official culture of Puerto Rico and its historical reality. Even though a major portion of the island's population descended from slaves or has some African blood, the Puerto Rican of myth, the protagonist of its literature, had exclusively been the *criollo* descendant of Spanish culture. One result of this dichotomy is the psychological distance between the two parallel cultures that evolved owing to the island's geographic and economic conditions: in the mountains, the *criollo* planted and sowed; on the flat, coastal plantations grew the sugar, and the *negro* cut the cane, the ex-slave having long been discouraged, including by law, from penetrating beyond the coast.[17]

By the early twentieth century, however, the rural *criollo* was already disappearing, giving way to an urban variety, especially in literature. Nevertheless, the myth of the *jíbaro* endured (and continues to this day). In 1926, the year after the publication of his first Afro-Antillean poem, in response to an interviewer on the existence of a creole poetry in Puerto Rico, Palés commented on the waning of the *jíbaro* model:

> Yes, a creole poetry definitely exists in Puerto Rico. What no longer exists is the creole. The humble hut, the sentimental and early rising country girl, the *camagüey* rooster, the feminine-toned, sensual small guitar, all this occupies so little space in our life, is so distant from us as the Eiffel Tower and Napoleon's white horse.[18]

Puerto Rico's clinging to its *criollo* myth is only part of an identity problem that antedates the Spanish-American War and the island's becoming a U.S. colony. In the nineteenth century, when other Latin American lands won independence and formed a national consciousness, Puerto Rico (as did Cuba) remained Spanish, a military base that had to play host to exiled Spaniards. Severe censorship and stringent tests of loyalty greatly affected Puerto Rico's notion of itself. Although a distinct sense of identity did express itself in an independence movement, Puerto Rican consciousness was actually born of two minds, divided between a *separatista* national model, which tellingly was also an abolition movement, and the *reformista* position, which advocated a culturally autonomous *patria chica*, not unlike a Spanish province.[19] Of these two postures, then, one sought the island's authenticity outright, incorporating freed slaves, and the other was uncertain of the benefits of freedom especially because of those Africans possibly roaming free. The example of Haiti, a land overrun by "barbarous" Africans who slaughtered whites, in fact, served to punctuate the Spanish government's warning to those islanders who contemplated separating from Spain.

In Palés's day, these two positions surfaced politically in the rising nationalist movement and culturally in Hispanism, a general identification of Puerto Rico with Spanish culture. Against the Anglo onslaught, these two movements seemed to be political and cultural factions in a common struggle to defend Puerto Rican culture, but Palés knew better. He, of course, was firmly a member of the cultural and political resistance, and one can infer

from his being prompted in 1936, the year of the outbreak of the
Spanish civil war, to publish *Tuntún* in 1937 as an act of solidarity
with Spanish kinship. Up to that time, Palés had not been especially interested in publishing his books. But that book has another purpose and its publication at that time also argues that
Palés was skeptical of Hispanism. While opposed to U.S. domination and Washington's campaign to Anglicize Puerto Rican society, he was equally opposed to the intelligentsia's using Spain to
blot out Puerto Rico's unique identity, a fear vindicated by the
subsequent reception of notable Spanish exiles: the eventual Nobel Laureate Juan Ramón Jiménez and the half-Puerto Rican cel-
list Pablo Casals soon became the centerpieces of Puerto Rican
cultural life. They also provided the hispanophile with prestigious
rejoinders to Palés's proposition that the island's defining spirit
was African.

That Palés perceived the mythic Iberianization of Puerto Rico
as a threat is evidenced in his change of attitude toward Spanish
poetry. In 1927, when asked his opinion of Spanish writing of the
day, Palés listed the familiar outstanding names from the Generation of '98. In 1932, with his own voice more clearly defined, he
specifically states his identification with three: "The strength of
the new Spanish poets—Lorca, Alberti, Villalón—is rooted in its
spiritually identifying with popular motives."[20] In these poets
Palés heard popular voices and a search for cultural authenticity.
They were his counterparts who would not impose Castile on the
Caribbean and instead celebrated the locality, as Palés himself
had been doing.

But Palés's respect of "los motivos populares" must be put into
the context of his stylistic complexity. This respect of the popular
prompted Palés to eliminate social register in subject or imagery
so that when we read his poems we find that the presumed jocu-
lar and vulgar can be read as seriously and the presumed important can be vulgarly treated. Secondly, Palés's focus on the
popular, by which he really also intended to say concrete reality,
was a way of counteracting a natural tendency in him to escape
to poetry, *sueño*. As this study will show, his poems record a
shuttling between a *sueño* and reality. And lastly, owing to his
stylized use of concrete reality, his popular elements do not become material of social documentary; rather, they generate elaborate conceits that Palés encodes in the subtleties of his style. He
paints a picture, the one that the populous can see, and simultaneously has painted others, at times so subtle as to become virtually private, escaping the casual reader.

Owing to this Palesian *conceptismo*, one can never be certain of having exhausted the nuances in his imagery. In the poem "Kalahari," Palés describes a day when he, hungover, obsessively reflected on the name of that desert, from which many of Puerto Rico's slaves presumably originated. Even though the poem "Kalahari" points to lush "cocoteros" ("coconut groves"), *The New Columbia Encyclopedia*, published in 1975, describes that desert as a region that, "covered largely by reddish sand, lies between the Orange and Zambezi rivers and is studded with dry lake beds. . . . Grass grows throughout the Kalahari in the rainy season, and some parts also support low thorn shrub and forest. Grazing and a little agriculture are possible in certain areas." Compare that description of the Kalahari with the region that Palés describes in his poem "Topografía":

Salitral blanquecino que atraviesa
roto de sed el pájaro;
con marismas resecas espaciadas
a extensos intervalos,
y un cielo fijo, inalterable y mudo,
cubriendo todo el ámbito.

Miedo. Desolación. Todo
duerme aquí sofocado
bajo la línea muerta que recorta
el ras rígido y firme de los campos.
Algunas cabras amarillas medran
en el rastrojo escaso,
y en la distancia un buey rumia su sueño
turbio de soledad y de cansancio.

[Hoary saltpeter birds fly over
frazzled with thirst;
with parched marshes spaced
one widely from the other,
a constant sky, unchangeable and mute,
doming every inch.

Fear. Desolation. Suffocation. Everything
here sleeps smothered
under the dead line that cuts
the countryside's hard, angular skyline.
A few yellow goats graze
on the sparse stubble,
and in the distance an ox chews his dream,
beset with solitude and fatigue.]

"Topografía," not published as part of the original *Tuntún*, belonged to the unpublished *Canciónes de la Vida Media*, which Palés described as a collection of poems on his hometown. That book was announced in 1925, which meant that it was written concurrently with the first Afro-Antillean poems, which included "Kalahari." Federico de Onís, for example, placed "Kalahari" among the poems of *Canciones de la Vida Media* and not among the Afro-Antillean poems, among which it appears in the Arce de Vázquez edition, and, in the 1926, Robles Pazo's selection in Madrid. De Onís's unique critical choice was obviously a reflection of his own interpretation of where the poem belonged. The most valuable point here is how these two poems cryptically complement one another. Clearly, within the same period Palés was preoccupied with his having arrived at a keen awareness of his middle age, his personal origins, the cyclical pattern of time, and the metaphysical essence of things. Knowing Palés's style and that the *Canciones de la Vida Media* and *Tuntún de Pasa y Grifería* were written concurrently, we can read them aware that, in some encoded way, the poems of one book are also contained, as transformations, in poems of the other. Thus, specifically in the case of "Topografía," we read anticipating more layers than the physical surface. The geographic parallels between its description of Palés's home geography and the description he likely read somewhere of "Kalahari" suggests that in addition to the island setting, the topography in question was also originally intended to encompass a familiar area in the unconscious past of his soul. With this in mind, we can appreciate the new richness of the line, in "Topografía": "Esta es toda mi historia" ["This is my entire history"].

The underlying unity of these two poems, one implicitly *blanco* and the other labeled as *negro*, illustrates the subject of this book: the thematic and stylistic unity underlying the diverse stages of Luis Palés Matos's poetry and antipoetry. Throughout his career, Palés reiterated his obsession with the frontier where the mundane touches the spiritual or metaphysical, which he perceived as the true essence of things. His poems therefore are structured to take the reader on a passage to a metaphysical realm and ultimately to an encounter with one of a number of imagistic representations of the essential that informs the soul of the individual, the collectivity, and the physical world. All his poems comply with that description, including the Afro-Antillean poems, because they all originate from Palés's sense that language, including "Boricua," has spiritual or metaphysical properties. In the breadth of his work, the poem is an altar and style is a liturgy that invokes the essence, what he called the "numen."

To fully appreciate Palés as innovator and thinker, then, we must do so in the course of deciphering his complex style, whose critical appreciation has been heretofore so superficial as to distort our perception of Palés and his worth. In 1960 Enrique Anderson Imbert and Eugenio Florit, although failing to connect Palés or any other poet to the radical changes transpiring in poetry at the time they were writing (their anthology did not include Parra), described Palés as "uno de los más originales de esta época" ("one of the most original [poets] of the period"). They saw in what they termed his "gran orquesta" an antipoetic quality, "un contracanto irónico" ("an ironic countersong") that, chronologically seen by them as an isolated case, they interpreted it as unique among writers of *poesía negra*:

> In his great orchestra one hears an ironic countersong; because Palés Matos is not black, being white, and smiles before the contrasts of both cultures, . . . In this ironic note, skepticism and refined melancholy of a cultured man, he is different precisely from others who work in the same genre of poetry.[21]

But Palés's "contracanto irónico" was also fresh to Latin American poetry in general, as it became evident when the following generation of poets used "ironía," "escepticismo," and "refinada melancolía" to express the attitudes of an age.

Unfortunately, the poet that Anderson Imbert's and Florit's words serve to describe really remains unknown to the literary world. In keeping with the convention of seeing the Caribbean and specifically Afro-inspired poetry in a distinct literary genealogy, critics who have investigated *poesía negra* have never placed it in the larger poetic context, limiting their look to comparisons with other *poesía negra* or turning Palés into a colorful and playful Caribbean poet of unsemantic imagery and catchy rhythms, with no discourse other than the one prefabricated by the reader's expectations. A number of critics, of course, have written on his work, but none has written extensively and those who have treated him invariably relied on the observations of Margot Arce de Vázquez, who never managed to grasp Palés's purpose or discourse and, in the question of style, never really got beyond an inventory of lexical patterns.

The closest thing to a deeper level investigation of Palés is a kind of psychological analysis of his having set out to denigrate

Puerto Rican letters by claiming that the defining spirit of the Caribbean soul, no matter what color body it inhabits, is African. Gustavo Agrait, for example, accused Palés of writing "black" poems because he was bored with Western civilization. The Afro-Antillean poems were merely the literary postures of a man too sophisticated to really believe the romanticism he was espousing:

> Luis Palés Matos, white, fine, civilized, refined, is at once a person disenchanted with civilization . . .

> The sophistry that the civilized represents over the virginal, the primitive, the ancestral, the pristene animal in man, doesn't appear to have the support of Palés the poet or Palés the man.[22]

According to this argument, the Afro-Antillean poems represented a passion for the exotic. Palés's phonological and rhythmic devices merely evoked a white man's anthropological dream of African people and landscapes and not the genuine thing. Inevitably, these critiques found it relevant to compare Palés's fantasy *poesía negra* with Nicolás Guillén's testimonial *poesía negra*, thus invoking the other convention of *poesía negra* as primarily sociopolitical documentation.

Palés's social consciousness, of course, concentrated on his culture's struggles with self-identity and authenticity, its penchant for self-denial, and its division into cultural classes. Some social and anthropological readings of his work have helped us with insights into that consciousness. But Palés was too rich and varied to be contemplated from that angle alone. By not approaching Palés by way of his poetics first, as both poet and antipoet of his day, that criticism never arrives at the extent and breadth of his true social consciousness or his inherently spiritual and philosophical obsessions. More important, that limited criticism has not only distorted our perception of the measure of the poet, it has ultimately reduced his stature. Consequently, our focused and fresh look must really begin with a review of that criticism standing between us and our full appreciation of Luis Palés Matos.

2

Palés Matos and His Critics

Luis Palés Matos began to receive important recognition in the summer of 1926, when the critics Federico de Onís and José Robles Pazos visited Puerto Rico. The following year, in *La Gaceta Literaria* in Madrid, Robles Pazos published "Un Poeta Borinqueño," which was illustrated with a selection of three poems, "Danza Caníbal" (an early title of "Candombe"), "Kalahari," and "Canción Festiva para ser Llorada" (Arce, 362). In his 1930 article in English, "A Puertorican Poet: Luis Palés Matos," Tomás Blanco cited the Spaniard, Angel Valbuena Prat, who described Palés's "Negroid poems as perfect," and also cited Amado Alonso, who credited Palés with possessing "the secret witchcraft of rhythm."[1]

Such weighty recognition from *la Madre Patria*, a major accomplishment for an island poet, prompted a generation of Hispanophilic Puerto Rican critics to respond, apparently now forced to verbalize their heretofore silent resentment of these *poemas negros*. For Palés Matos had not merely begun to play around with African sounds; the Afro-Antillean poems were predicated on his cultural vision of the Caribbean, and for this Palés was accused of misrepresenting Puerto Rican culture. One reviewer, Luis Antonio Miranda, countered with a racist, pun-laden article, "El Llamado Arte Negro No Tiene Vinculación en Puerto Rico" ("No Basis for the So-Called Black Art in Puerto Rico").[2] The following year Graciany Miranda Archilla published "La Broma de Una Poesía Prieta en Puerto Rico" ("The Joke of a Darkie Poetry in Puerto Rico"), another article whose title summarizes its content.[3]

Those two articles represented, of course, the most extreme and extroverted reaction, but that Palés had provoked the intelligentsia by poking at a sensitive nerve is also evident in the critiques of Palés's most devoted critic, Margot Arce de Vázquez, who, in a more moderate tone, expressed the same sense of effrontery, or at least the feeling that Palés had exaggerated the African contribution to Puerto Rican culture. In a 1931 lecture

"Los Poemas Negros de Luis Palés Matos" ("The Black Poems of
Luis Palés Matos") she wrote: "One cannot deny the influence of
black culture in the life of the Caribbean, but it seems somewhat
risky to affirm that it is the characterizing influence."[4]

We read Arce's words keeping in mind that Puerto Ricans were
steeped in an identity crisis brought on by the United States'
possession of the island. Three years after Arce's lecture, Antonio S. Pedreira published his *Insularismo* (1934), a major essay that
attempts to define the collective Puerto Rican personality. Like
Arce and the island's intelligentsia of their day, Pedreira argued
that the seed of Puerto Rican culture was European and specifically Spanish and that if Puerto Rico's soul was to survive the
spiritual drought that came with the materialist Northerners it
would have to drink again of Spain's humanist waters. In other
words, through *Insularismo* Pedreira expressed an earlier influence of *arielismo*, a continental response to Yankee cultural and
economic influence. Nevertheless, Pedreira did acknowledge
Palés as a major figure in a generation of poets that represented
Puerto Rican poetry's recovery from a long "pulmonía poética"
("poetic pneumonia") in the nineteenth century. Pedreira here
praised Palés's originality in writing "poesía negra." But given
Pedreira's patent racism, expressed in other sections of his essay,
as well as his Westernist motif, one must deduce that he disagreed with the grandiose claims Palés was making of the African
spirit as definer of the Antillean identity. Not identifying Palés as
his interlocutor, Pedreira follows up his praise of the poet with
an enigmatic paragraph:

> Something has been discussed in our days about the sense (or non-
> sense) of an Antillean art that synchronizes the spiritual movement
> of the Greater Antilles, and it appears to me that the first thing is to
> establish what are Cuba, Santo Domingo, and Puerto Rico. In order
> to use the general accent, as one, the particular accent of each island
> must first be defined; after the tone and the dimension of each people
> are made clear, then look for the expressive synthesis of the Antillean
> triangle. Approaching the question any other way will only end up
> being a detriment to the overall goal.[5]

Pedreira apparently distrusted Palés's proselytizing an intuitive
summation of an Antillean spirit before giving evidence of a more
anthropologically valid observation of each island in its particular-
ity. His response, of course, doesn't deny Palés's point and simply
defends his own more scientific approach, evident throughout
Insularismo, of putting Puerto Rican culture under a microscope.

One also detects, however, an intellectual filibustering. Not denying that there is a single defining spirit, on the one hand, Pedreira postpones conceding that the islands do share a spiritual oneness until after more investigation is done into their distinct "accent," "tone," and "dimension." What that means is unclear, although it suggests a cultural analysis using proven techniques. *Spirit* cannot be measured using anthropological methods; spirit is the purview of a medium, artistic or spiritual. Pedreira's response to Palés, then, illustrates through reflex reaction exactly what Pedreira himself condemned as a flaw in the Puerto Rican personality. While he laments the narrow, *insularismo* mindset that Puerto Ricans have inherited over the years, his response to Palés is given strictly from the viewpoint of the creole, shutting out the island's other cultural components. In this, beside compromising his objectivity as an observer, Pedreira illustrated the kind of denial that Palés attacked in celebrating the island's African roots and its true regional context.

Although Pedreira and Palés stand in direct contradiction in their interpretation of Puerto Rican culture, both writers express the common thematic preoccupation that the destiny of Puerto Rico has been determined by the island's inability to confront harsh reality and take charge of it and that the instrument of denial has been its circumventing or euphemistic language. From the opening line of Pedreira's preface, the failure to confront reality becomes the leitmotiv of *Insularismo*: "These words will omit that flattering tone that our complacency has created to measure our reality" (Pedreira, 25). In the chapter "Nuestro Retoricismo," although underscoring that all Latin America shares the character flaw of "retoricismo," he ascribes the cultivation of circumlocution in Puerto Rico to the conditions imposed by Spanish oppression: "We, who have always lived immersed in grammar, have never been able to call things by their proper name" (Pedreira, 113).

Pedreira's words invoke Palés's earlier definition of his island, referred to in the rare singular form "Antilla," in "Canción Festiva para Ser Llorada":

> Aristocracia de dril
> donde la vida resbala
> sobre frases de natilla
> y suculentas metáforas.
> Estilización de costas
> a cargo de entecas palmas.
> Idioma blando y chorreoso
> —mamey, cacao, guanábana—.
> . . . .

sólo a veces Don Quijote,
por chiflado y musaraña,
de tu maritornería
construye una dulcineada.

[White linen aristocracy
where life is a glide
over custard phrases
and succulent metaphors.
A drafting of coastlines
penned by languid palms.
A bland and dripping language
—*mamey, cacao, guanábana*—.
. . . .
only at times Don Quixote,
being daft and in a cloud,
from your Maritornes whoring
fabricates a Dulcinea.]

Unfortunately, as Pedreira spoke of white culture and Palés's poems were presumably *negros*, critics have not picked up on this common theme. Nevertheless, it is key to understanding one of the motives underlying Palés Matos's graviting to "boricua" as his writing language. Different from the *criollo's* formal, cautious, oblique Spanish that Pedreira perceived as corrupted by its ingrained bent toward *retoricismo*, another branch of the island's language was concrete and forthright: the informal language of unprestigious speech, "boricua," which was loaded with African-derived words.

The counterpoint between formal *criollo* Spanish and informal "boricua" reflected two wholly contradictory ways of perceiving the world and raises a possible theory about how Palés was affected by coming upon that realization. In his non-Afro-Antillean phase, Palés himself was oblique about putting forth his own poetry, taking little interest (after his first youthful effort) in publishing completed books. With *Tuntún* Palés's appeared to follow the lesson of forthrightness, an anti-*criollo* expression, of publishing the book that did the unthinkable in Puerto Rico: frankly pronouncing by his poems that "boricua" was an enriched version of Spanish spoken on the island and that its being Afro-Antillean in spirit and flavor was what made Puerto Ricans who they are. As an antidote to *retoricismo*, Afro-Antilleanism, then, was also the anti-matter to the Hispanist intellectuals who turned to Spain in search of a cultural model, a situation made especially ironic by the probability that the Hispanists's clinging fast to Spain was partially in response to the Anglo-American's racial perception of Puerto Rico.

Understated and unspoken, race has always been a sensitive component of the debate over the island's political status and cultural identity. Because Palés Matos dared to claim that Puerto Rico is half-Spanish and half-African, he irritated tender sensibilities, and therefore his poetry provoked the counterattack of island conventions that played down African culture in Puerto Rico's official myths. Thus, even though less blatant in their racism than Graciany Miranda Archilla, the more serious critics elegantly evinced the same racial attitudes. Margot Arce de Vázquez equated *negro* with things crude and grotesque and took for granted that Palés did too. She therefore routinely categorized images under such headings as "grotesco" to establish points of comparisons she presumed Palés himself was making. Tomás Blanco wrote of the Afro-Antillean poems in a condescending tone, employing the diminutive form "negrito" when referring to the black *caribeño*. In his article, "En Familia," for instance, he differentiated between Palés's fictive "negro, negro," (Blanco's way of saying "African") and those "negritos muy nuestros" whom Blanco saw as true representations of Afro-Caribbean peoples: "There also reside other darkies, other likeable darkies, very much ours, very much of the Caribbean, in Palés's poems."[6]

In the years between 1926 and the publication of *Tuntún de Pasa y Grifería* in 1937, other *poesía negra*, by both white and black poets, emerged throughout Anglo and Latin America, creating a body of work that was rediscovered in the sixties with the emergence of African Americans in the United States. In Spanish, however, in the sixties, Nicolas Guillén became the standard by which Palés's *poesía afroantillana* was measured. Compared to the popular, folk or spoken style of Guillén's poems, Palés appeared to be playing bourgeois word games at the expense of black culture. Even worse, because Guillén was black, his work was perceived by critics as resulting from authentic experience as compared to Palés's poems, which depicted Africans, to quote Tomás Blanco, "inspired by explorers and ethnographers. . . ." (*The American Mercury*, 75).

Another reason for Guillén's preeminence, aside from the worth of his work, was the inseparable preconceptions that *poesía negra* had to give voice to "lo popular" and therefore had to be exemplary as social realism. Margot Arce de Vázquez harbored both those preconceptions and consequently measured Palés's use of black imagery against the folkloric monologues of the Cubans, Guillén and Emilio Ballagas:

> Luis Palés Matos is a cultured poet, or more accurately, a baroque cultured-style poet. The artifice of his poetry reveals itself in the truly Gongorine care that he devotes to form and metaphor. He shuns the popular poetic modes; interprets black things in the mode of the skeptical and civilized white man. In this he is different from Nicolás Guillén and Emilio Ballagas. These poets rely on authentic popular forms and try to translate realistically, not superrealistically, the spirit of the black race. . . . They see the black from within and as black" (Arce, 50–51).

Because Guillén and Ballagas used "authentic popular forms," they saw "the black from within and as black." In other words, Palés's being "a cultured poet" makes him incapable of being insightful about, or even being sympathetic about African Caribbean culture. This illogic aside, the discussion itself is largely academic because Palés's purpose was overlooked in the assumption that he had set out to do what Ballagas and Guillén later presumably perfected.

Indicative of the durability of Arce's comment, almost three decades later Nilita Vientós Gastón would make the same comparison, also implying by her logic that being "culto" and seeing black culture as the majority of the other poets saw it are mutually exclusive possibilities:

> Palés is not, despite his having worked with black themes and the popularity it has brought him, a popular poet. Quite the contrary. He is, as many of his critics have observed, a cultured poet, baroque in form, incapable by his temperament—that uses irony to camouflague feelings—of perceiving the black like most of the other poets who have worked in the genre.[7]

Arce's original counterpoint between *lo culto* and *lo popular* in fact became the stock critical assumption of the entire first generation of Palesian critics, who adopted this model in their discussion of the breadth of Palés's poetry. Referring to the Afro-Antillean poems as intellectual exercises, this criticism counterposed them with his "white" poems as expressions of lived experience. Arce's "culto/popular" dichotomy, then, was a variant on Blanco's "negro negro" (abstract)/"negrito muy nuestro" (real) dichotomy cited earlier. Consequently, save for a few exceptions "exceptionally local in subject," to quote Blanco, the

Afro-Antillean poems were usually discussed as examples of Palés's phonological virtuosity, while the "white" poems were more apt to be treated as his most personal or significantly social statements. Note that Blanco, assuming nothing visceral is contained in Palés's look at the Caribbean, failed to see the irony in Palés's handling of tragedy in "Canción Festiva para Ser Llorada," of which Blanco highlighted Palés's "light and colorful mood":

> Among them there is one exceptionally local in subject, "Canción Festiva par Ser Llorada" . . . dealing with the grotesque tragedy of the Antilles in a light and colorful mood." (Blanco, 75)

Such preconceptions about Palés by the first generation of island critics went on to influence critics from outside of Puerto Rico. Enrique Anderson Imbert, for example, converted the *culto/popular* dichotomy into one of the superficial and the profound:

> The reading of his book *Poesía 1915–1956*— published in 1957—shows a complete Palés Matos that doesn't remain on the surface of black themes, rather that he plunges into a more profound, esencial, complex and enduring poetry. Then one understands that those black poems (see "Black Dance") were mere episodes in the expression of a sad look at elemental life and the dispersion of nothingness (see "The Call"). (Enrique Anderson Imbert, *Historia de la Literatura Latinoamericana*, 6th ed, (Mexico: Fondo de Cultural Económica, 1954), 189).

One cannot help commenting on Anderson Imbert's ambiguous use of the phrase "the surface of black themes" which isn't followed up by a statement of Palés's acquiring a deeper perception of that theme, rather it goes on to make the point that Palés progressed to more profound poems having nothing to do with negritude.

In another example, Jean Franco, in *The Modern Culture of Latin America*, briefly discusses Palés, quoting from two poems to illustrate her comments. She writes: "Palés Matos's poems are amusing and playful, and evoke a lazy tropical and sensual atmosphere in which the Negro song is an invitation to curl up in the womb and dream.[8] This was Franco's way of introducing her citation of the last stanza of "Pueblo Negro." The "curling up" by the reader should presumably take place in the maternal "ú profunda del diptongo fiero" ("the savage dipthong's deep *u*-sound"), an image at the end of that poem.

Perhaps because she was expecting something more playful, Franco completely missed that Palés frequently expressed his sense of time and history through his concomitant sense of linguistic diachrony and synchrony. As will be demonstrated later in this chapter, "Pueblo Negro" is encoded to keep the reader conscious of the frontier between reality and dream, departure and return, past and present, dualisms that all converge in Palés's sense of the crystallization of time in language. The "ú profunda" is a phonological element charged with the same evocative power that Palés explores in his poem about the recurring word "Kalahari."

Of course, Franco's and Anderson Imbert's respective histories cover too many authors for these critics to be expected to reinterpret every author they chose to highlight. In Palés's case, the first generation of his critics were the ones responsible for designing the original mold into which Franco and Anderson attempted to stuff Palés's poems. In this way, whether wittingly or not, they propagated an interpretation that marked Palés's major work, *Tuntún de Pasa y Grifería*, as superficial. Take as an example one of Tomás Blanco's remarks, originally written in English. After introducing Muna Lee's translation of half of "San Sabás" and his own translation of "Pueblo," Blanco commented that Palés "best work, the oncoming of his poetical maturity, the attainment of real originality, dates only from the publication of his first Negroid poem . . ." (Blanco, 75), to which he dedicated two brief paragraphs and an eight-line translated quotation, of the stanza cited earlier, from "Canción Festiva," referring to Don Quixote and with no "Negroid" imagery. Blanco epitomizes the pattern of critical writings on Palés: much either subjective praise or chastisement supported by little substantive textual analysis.

In the late sixties and seventies, a new generation accused Palés of having taken a reactionary position in the face of Puerto Rican social reality and of being a racist. Like the earlier critics, younger ones also identified "negro" with "popular" and measured Palés's success by the degree to which his poems were socially realistic. As in the early sixties, Guillén continued to be the standard of perfection and the background that put Palés's poetry in doubt was the social consciousness that prevailed after the Cuban revolution. The poet, José Manuel Torres Santiago, published an open letter in the poetry journal he edited, *Guajana*,[9] considered the publication of the generation of the sixties in Puerto Rico, in which he responded to statements made by the novelist, José Luis González, on a number of subjects, including González's defense of Palés Matos.

Torres, who eventually acknowledged that Palés's later work

"in a few poems improves upon the political and racial positions of his earlier work" argues that, far from being politically or racially revolutionary, as González had asserted, Palés "held very conscious political positions that although it hurts to point them out were colonizing." Disregarding the significance of Palés's evolving consciousness, which Torres himself acknowledged, his chief complaint was that Palés was imperialist-minded: "it is the empire that penetrates his conscience and not the struggle of the people at the level it finds itself." Lacking a more substantive explication of what Torres meant and taking into account Palés's wholly anti-imperialist discourse, one can only surmise that Torres really was complaining that Palés did not use the Marxist language that would have patently involved him in the popular struggle, another way of complaining that Palés was no Guillén. Finally, in a statement on the role of Palés's poetry in affirming the African contribution to Puerto Rico's national culture, Torres disagreed with critic, Arcadio Díaz Quiñones, that Palés's poetry serves this function: "For Palés, the black is a savage incapable of being civilized."

In 1969, Manuel Maldonado Denis published a Marxist interpretation of Puerto Rican social history in which he discusses Palés, repeating the same observations made by Arce, Blanco and Vientós Gastón over the course of four decades. Furthermore, he explicitly separated the issue of "negritude" from that of "our reality": "But his interest in 'negritude' takes him through the path of evading our reality." Ultimately, Palés is compared to Guillén, whom Maldonado Denis condescendingly assessed as a *black* who had a "radical social vision," and whom Denis was implicitly comparing not to Palés but to Palés's black, "who only dances and fornicates and ends up grotesquely imitating his white oppressors."[10]

The contrasts between Palés and Guillén shouldn't overshadow the things they have in common, but to illustrate the numerous similarities would require another chapter not germane to this study. For a more thorough treatment, the reader should see Mónica Mansour's *La Poesía Negrista*.[11] The problem is not that these poets should be compared, but that one should be treated as a standard for the other. Their being poets of different races in similar racist societies naturally results in major stylistic differences in their poetry. Guillén's poetry, whether of his individual or collective persona, is quite naturally a testimonial poetry while Palés's Afro-Antillean poems logically have the character of meditations, of essays about a cultural strain that he and his populace spiritually identify with, but which his literature and formal language have treated as exotic.

Like Guillén, Palés was born into a declining society that denied that it was also composed of African ingredients. Guillén inquired into his blood, his grandfather's surnames and Cuban history and lamented for his lost self, bleached out by white culture. Palés, haunted by Puerto Rico's history that harbors the same racial secret, invoked the hidden African "numen" from the temple in which it resides, in Puerto Rico's language. Guillén gave a voice to the marginalized Afro-Cuban sector of his island; lacking that anger, Palés laments the condition of Afro-Antilleans, but celebrates their spiritual legacy to his island and its Caribbean context, regardless of color. The difference between the two would appear to be that Guillén's poems sprang from a blood link to Africa and Palés's poems sprang from a curiosity about his spiritual ties to Africa, leaving their white author's sincerity, motives and intentions wholly open to interpretation. Those who perceive Palés as a racist or are offended by his assertions about the island's culture are also questioning the degree to which Palés felt black in his own soul. They fail or simply refuse to see that, lacking the immediate blood referents, such as a surname or a grandfather, he reflected on his discovered spiritual legacy through his language and, as this study endeavors to prove by its analysis, stylistically responded to that encounter exactly as he did to spiritual encounters in his non-Afro-Antillean poems.

His Afro-Antillean poems, in fact, evolved from the discourse that he had been developing since his earliest poems, on the nature of poetry and the workings of his soul. How did poetry flourish in him? he repeatedly inquired in diverse imagistic reiterations. His body lived a tedious existence, like the man in the wheel chair in "Tic-Toc," but inside he felt the depths of "El Pozo" ("The Well"), a medium to eternity and psychic strength. The pattern repeated itself when he contemplated his social context. The deadness he felt in his body was inseparable from the society in which he grew up, a spiritually declining criollo-based society ("Pueblo") and in a geographically arid region ("Topografía"). And yet at a point in his life he became conscious that, under the dead society that routinely belittled the black culture on the fringes of its consciousness, another energy had been secretly inspiriting the atmosphere of the land, energizing him without his realizing it. His becoming mature meant his defying the criollo myth and accepting the truth of another legacy. As observed earlier, his overlapping mature books, Canciones de la vida media and

Tuntún de pasa y grifería, respectively referred to as "white" and "black," were written during the same period, reflecting his inner drama. Palés's groping explains the contradictions that strike us when we read poems like the pessimistic "Pueblo" from *Canciones* and the exuberant "Danza Negra" from *Tuntún.*

A similar inconsistency is even evident in the stages of development within the context of the Afro-Antillean poems. In a prefiguration of *Tuntún,* "Esta Noche He Pasado" ("Tonight I Have Passed") which appears in the Arce de Vázquez edition among the poems of the unpublished *El Palacio en Sombras* ("The Palace in Shadows," 1918–1919), Palés walks white-minded through his town's black quarter. Already the play on *pasa* (kinky hair) and *pasar* is apparent in the title and in the refrain "Esta noche he pasado por un pueblo de negros" ["Tonight I have passed through a black town."] But here it's a pun that more obviously tilts toward being racist, in harmony with the attitude of the persona, who has a pathetic view of the black people he observes as a vanquished people:

> ¡No! La pompa jocunda de estas tribus ha muerto.
> Les queda una remota tristeza cuadrumana,
> una pasión ardiente por los bravos alcoholes,
> el odio milenario del blanco, y la insaciable
> lujuria de las toscas urgencias primitivas.

> [No! The cheerful pomp of those tribes has died.
> All that remains is a remote four-hooved sadness,
> a sweltering passion for strong liquor,
> an ancient hatred of whites, and the unsated
> indulgence of raw, primitive drives.]

That stanza's opening negation is in response to his own imagination, which in the previous stanza had taken flight, idealizing or romanticizing or seeing an earlier greatness. However one wishes to interpret the transition and the poem's naive, racist motives, poetically speaking, in the parenthetical stirrings of his imagination, within this very "white" poem is where his Afro-Antillean consciousness begins to emerge:

> El espíritu cafre de las lujurias roncas
> y los bruscos silencios huracanados, flota
> sobre este barrio oscuro . . . (Y doy a imaginarme
> golpes secos de gongo, gritos, y un crudo canto
> lleno de diptongueantes guturaciones ñáñigas . . .

Alguna bayadera del Congo está ahora
destorciendo el elástico baile de la serpiente
dentro del agrio círculo de brujos y guerreros,
todos llenos de horribles tatuajes, mientras arden
las fogosas resinas, y el fuego, rey del día,
dora la res que se asa sobre tizones rojos).

[The savage spirit of hoarse-voiced lusts
and fierce, hurricane-force silences hover
over this dark ward . . . (And I begin to imagine
staccato drumbeats, screams, and a crude chant
full of diphthongizing *ñáñigo* gutturals . . .
Some Congo bayadere must now be uncoiling
the elastic dance of the serpent
in the caustic ring of witchdoctors and warriors,
their entire bodies grotesquely tatooed, while the flaming
resins burn, and fire, king of the day,
golden roasts the beef over red wood).]

This parenthetical diversion is consistent with the consciousness of surface/inner lines throughout Palés's poetry, and is importantly reiterated at the end of the poem:

Ante este pueblo negro y estas casas de podre
y esta raza ya hundido para siempre, yo tengo
la visión de espantosos combustibles; la brea,
el diamante, el carbón, el odio y la montaña . . .

[Before this black town and these houses of pus
and this race now sunken forever, I visualize
spontaneous combustibles: tar,
diamond, carbon, hatred and the mountain . . .]

The submerged "pueblo negro," a homonym of "black people," which is before and outside of him, also evokes from his imagination forms of energy. Over the years, this subtler posture will become explicit, as specifically in "Pueblo Negro" ("Black Town") in which the town is in a remote vision but always inside him, in his language, and instead of seeing that black race as pathetic and beyond him, he affirms that these energetic evocations originate from inside him and from the same spiritual fount.

Those critics who have accused Palés of being a racist have exhibited ignorance of the significance of Palés's evolution and the consistency of his style. In his *Narciso Descubre su Trasero: el Negro en la Cultura Puertorriqueña (Narcissus Discovers his Rearend:*

The Black Man in Puerto Rican Culture), Isabelo Zenón Cruz accuses Palés of employing racist stereotypes in *Tuntún.* He especially chastises Palés's depicting black people, whether in Africa or in the Caribbean, as sexual maniacs:

> Let us look at Palés Matos for being the most important poet who has treated the theme of the black man in his poetry. Concerning the Palesian notion of the sexuality of the black, almost all the most important critics coincide in that he attributes to them a "high sexual temperature." Very few, nevertheless have censured him for this, although they have for other reasons.[12]

The expression "high sexual temperature," Cruz goes on to explain, comes from Margot Arce de Vázquez, who is also accused of propagating the stereotype of black supersexuality. Furthermore, Cruz accuses Palés Matos of sympathizing with the notion that Africans are by nature savages:

> He believes, besides, that the authentic African is a savage incapable of being civilized; moreover, he suggests [the black man] has never known anything like civilization. (Cruz, 133)

The speciousness of these assertions notwithstanding, some of Cruz's objections are valid, especially in reference to the poems "Esta Noche He Pasado" ("Tonight I Have Passed"), "Lagarto Verde" ("Green Alligator"), and "Elegía del Duque de la Mermelada" ("Elegy of the Duke of Marmelade") as being especially offensive: "Esta Noche," as discussed above, for being a clearly racist poem, and the other two because in them the Haitian aristocrats are described in simian metaphors. These poems, especially the latter two, most typify Puerto Rican racist humor of Palés's generation. Using these poems as examples, out of context, one can indeed make a case that Palés was simply a racist.

On the other hand, his work records the stages of a growing consciousness that culminated in his vision of the *mulata* myth in "Mulata-Antilla" ("Mulatto Woman-Island"). Thus, we must read the three poems that Cruz cites or any others that show Palés to be a racist within the context of his personal evolution, as illustrated earlier, in the contrast between "Esta Noche He Pasado" and "Pueblo Negro." In the case of the simian metaphors in both "Lagarto Verde" and "Elegía del Duque de la Mermelada," Cruz disregards that in these poems Palés employs the convention of the mimicking ape. As will be shown later, while animal metaphors abound in Palés's poetry, the simian metaphors in those two poems satirize the mental and cultural colonization of Henri Christophe and his court.

Cruz's other indictment, the hypersexual depiction of Africans, is contradicted by many other poems that his critique never takes into consideration. Palés ascribed this hypersexuality to all the Caribbean; a cult to sensuality is a defining characteristic of the region—that un-Protestant and un-Catholic, spiritually free African spirit, according to the poet, is Africa's saving endowments to the Antilles. Palés celebrates this sexual force in a number of poems, most notably "Mulata-Antilla" and "Plena del Menéalo" ("Shake it *Plena*"), and reiterates it in nonracial imagery in "El Gallo") ("The Rooster") in which a rooster becomes the phallic potency symbolizing the Antilles. It is that cult to sensuality that differentiates the Puerto Rican from the Protestant Yankee occupier, making that sexual force, in Palés's vision, a numinous expression of Puerto Rico's true identity and thus a defense against the threat of annexation. In the "Plena del Menéalo" ("Shake It Up *Plena*"), an African-derived Puerto Rican dance, the "plena," symbolizes the continuing uniqueness that will save the island from Uncle Sam:

> Mientras bailes, no hay quien pueda
> cambiarte el alma y la sal.
> Ni agapitos por aquí,
> ni místeres por allá.
>
> [While you dance, none exists
> who can change your soul and salt.
> Neither *Agapitos* from down here,
> nor Misters from up there.][13]

The dancer is "la Antilla," Puerto Rico itself. Surely Arce de Vázquez herself would have considered Palés's exhortation to "menéalo, menéalo" ("shake it, shake it") as much an image of lasciviousness as is found in "Majestad Negra" ("Black Majesty") or "Elegía del Duque de la Mermelada" ("Elegy of the Duke of Marmelade") and here the poem cannot be accused of celebrating a racial stereotype.

That European culture has conventionally portrayed Africans as sensual or hypersexual as evidence of racial inferiority is true but Palés is a poor example of that convention at work. Palés was quite aware that the West frowns on what it regards as "primitive" sensuality and that its absence in Western culture is interpreted as proof of the white society's intellectual superiority. He also knew that, consistent with that tradition, the *criollo* half of Puerto Rican and Caribbean society responded predictably to Afro-Caribbeans. But Palés's argument is that no matter what the *criollo* society wants to believe, their being *caribeños* means that they are not just in the Caribbean; the Caribbean is also in them, imparting to them its cult to sensuality that routinely expresses itself in its music, its popular speech and, in short, all forms of expression that sets them apart from Spain and other branches of Latin America. That cult to sensuality, Palés insisted, came from the African energy it enjoys, an ancestry that liberates the Caribbean of squeamish Western taboos and the need to identify with European exhaustion. Like the declining West, the declining Creole society lacked that vitality and was therefore prepared to surrender to Yankee culture or its idealization of a bygone Spanish culture. In contrast, Afro-Caribbean culture possessed great numinous, including procreative, resources that can be the seed of Puerto Rico's liberation.

In sum, to pick away at poems out of that context, mindless of Palés ironic style, or only at poems with images of African and Afro-Caribbean people, fails to establish anything. For here is where Cruz, like many others, misreads Palés's Afro-Antillean poems. They are not about black people or white people, real or fictive, but about the obsessive and continual encounter of a white persona with a black heritage and the images of it in the soul of his language, images that range from the ridiculously racist to those that are sublime. This includes ironically assuming the poses programmed into his language, from the "civilized" to the renegade. Defending that sense of encounter is the focus of Arcadio Díaz Quiñones's response to the accusations that Palés was a racist and lacking a social consciousness.[14] In it, Díaz argues that the Afro-Antillean poems belong to the second phase of Palés's development, in which he begins to acquire a social awareness:

> It's in this second phase that the poet feels the need to learn and communicate the values of his culture, which will be the basis of the commitment the group takes on. In order to refresh his creative energy he had to return to cultural sources, to the roots, to thus arrive at an extreme tension of consciousness. A grave problem then presented itself: that a denied and distorted culture doesn't enjoy prestige. Even worse: there is a counterpropaganda that wants to impede the emergence of that cultural consciousness, to deny it or destroy it. (Díaz, 14)

Díaz cites the tree image that Palés employs to structure the contents of *Tuntún* as generally representing the stages of transition within the poet's social phase:

Afterwards follow three parts that the poet titles "Trunk," "Branch," "Flower." Interpreted generally and unrigorously, "Trunk" refers to the ancestral, African things in their purest state: dance, rhythm, temperament. In "Branch," he gathers the poems that deal with the results of resettling black people in the Caribbean. "Flower" groups the ironic poems, in which Palés eulogizes Puerto Rico, the racially mixed Antilles, and describes the tropical landscape. (Díaz, 15)

Díaz concurs with Palés that the last of these stages represents the blossoming of his consciousness because in that phase he arrived at his poetic symbol of the Antilles: *la mulata*, the heroine of the Antillean drama, "the synthesis of the people and land to which she belongs" (Díaz, 20). Embodying the Caribbean's *mulatez*, or racial mixture, her body regenerates its true spirit. In her, Palés saw the temple of the Caribbean's numen and a cultural bulwark against the danger of Anglo-Americanization. Equally as important, according to Díaz, the *mulata* fulfilled Palés's need to "affirm the Antillean will and provoke a renascence of its culture" (Díaz, 20). For, ultimately, Díaz emphasizes, Palés's aim was to create an image that was simultaneously cultural and political:

Palés's Afro-Antillean poetry is unintelligible if one doesn't take into account that Palés attempts to describe and at the same time unmask Puerto Rican society, with the objective of proposing a liberating design for the future. In that sense Palés' poetry transcends the reality and clashes at the same time with the prevailing social order. His poetry isn't a mere somber prediction of Antillean reality, nor is it a refuge or escape for the author, rather he is firmly anchored in history when he denounces the disorder of a social reality that does not allow a human collectivity that has a self-consciousness to express and develop itself: "This is the mandingue night / when something new is born" ("Bombo, p. 229"). It's an invitation to a rupture, a definite cutting off, a call, an invitation to the collectivity, to the burning island, to fulfill the transformation of the society. . . . (Díaz, 23)

Besides answering the postsixties critics, Díaz's article makes two valuable contributions: first, it introduces the idea of a Palesian sense of scheme as essential to a proper reading of Palés's poems; second, in contrast to the presixties critics, Díaz actually discusses the discourse of the Afro-Antillean poems, acknowledging their having an intellectual purpose.

Another critic who defends Palés against the accusations that he was a racist is the Cuban, Raúl Hernández Novás. In his introduction to *Poesía*, a volume of selected poems by Palés issued by Casa de las Américas, Hernández differentiates between the racist intellectual conventions that figured in Palés's formation and his actually being a racist himself. According to Hernández, Palés committed the mistake of accepting the proverbial dichotomy that supposedly divides Latin America: civilization and barbarism. By accepting this, Hernández says, Palés unwittingly accepted its corresponding set of stereotypes.[15] But Hernández errs in asserting that Palés wrote of two worlds, black and white, with the latter civilized and the former barbarian. Hernández himself got caught in the linguistic trap of thinking of these poems as *poesía negra*. *Tuntún de Pasa y Grifería* is about a mingling of black and white genius in the Caribbean, as Palés describes Puerto Rico in "Ten con Ten" ("Neither This Nor That"): "una mitad española / y otra mitad africana" ["One half Spanish, / the other African"]. Hernández himself indirectly retracts his original assertion of Palés's mistake by noting that he is best understood if the reader accepts that by white is meant the colonizer and by black the Antillean cultural character:

> We understand the sense of Palés' work better if by the "white" world to which he alludes we take to mean the colonizing, aggressor "civilization," and by "black," or more accurately, "mulatto," the whole Antillean culture and character. (Hernández Novás, xxiii)

Most of Hernández's observations and conclusions coincide with Díaz Quiñones's, who is not quoted.[16] Among the coincidences between those two critical interpretations, the most important for the purpose of this analysis is Hernández's observing the importance of understanding Palés's consciousness of encounter. In the course of responding to Nilita Vientós Gastón's critique that Palés's fictive "black is an abstract being," for example, Hernández refers to Palés's consciousness of encounter:

> even in the context of a single poem we witness a struggle between realism and idealization, between "the observed"—as Vientós Gastón would say—or the "truly lived"—as the poet himself expressed—and "what fantasy adds to these things." (Hernández Novás, xiv)

Among Palés's earliest critics, only Margot Arce de Vázquez wrote with an emphasis on his language and style. These discussions are found in three essays: "Los Poemas Negros de Luis Palés Matos" ("The Black Poems of Luis Palés Matos"), "Los Adjetivos en 'Danza Negra' de Luis Palés Matos" ("The Adjectives in 'Danza Negra'" by Luis Palés Matos"), "Tres Pueblos Negros: Algunas Observaciones sobre el Estilo de Luis Palés Matos"

("Three Black Towns: Some Observations on the Style of Luis Palés Matos"). The first, "Los Poemas Negros de Luis Palés Matos,"[17] identifies and very generally discusses two stylistic features: that of "suggestiveness" and "an imitative rhythm" that combine to create his poem's particular atmosphere. Except for a few quotations and a catalogue of especially evocative or onomatopoetic words that Palés employs, however, Arce provides few noteworthy examples.

More substantive is her study "Los Adjetivos en 'Danza Negra' de Luis Palés Matos" ("The Adjectives in 'Danza Negra' by Luis Palés Matos," *Impresiones*, 61–76), which is divided into three sections: an introductory descriptive part devoted to simple adjectives, a short listing of adjectival phrases ("sol de hierro," "islas de betún," etc.), and conclusions. Her treatment of the simple adjectives lists the denotations and possible connotations of the individual modifiers, including some references to sounds and rhythms of special interest. The modifying phrases are given the same treatment. She essentially takes an inventory of the quantity, distribution, position, and classification of adjectives (into "pure adjectives," "complex" or "metaphorical"). Throughout, these are treated as if they were simply words in a dictionary and not parts of a poem in which they might serve a highly specialized function. Arce isolates "negra," for example, from the longer adjectival string "danza negra de Fernando Póo" and gives a brief list of connotations evoked by the word "negra." This is questionable, especially since Palés's line reads: "Es la danza negra de Fernando Póo." Every word beyond "Es" is part of the predicate nominative, so that the "danza" is not just negra but "de Fernando Póo" as well. The full semantic significance of this image might have escaped Arce whose brief note on "de Fernando Póo" fails to inform that it was a small island off the northwestern coast of Africa and that it was famous for its slave mills. By separating that prepositional phrase from the rest of the predicate nominative, she misses that, among other things, the "danza negra" is the dance of the enslaved. And related to that example, Arce says nothing of the intentional ambiguity of "de hierro" ("of iron") in the "sol de hierro" metaphor that, besides being an obvious image of an oppressive molten-metal sun, also refers to the white-hot branding iron.

In another example, Arce describes the evocations of the word "gordo" in the image "ritmo gordo":

> Firmness of tact and form applied to sound . . . *Gordo* evokes a torpid, repetitive, sensual rhythm; a rhythm of greasy bodies; a rhythm that

lacks harmony and beauty. The assessment is tinged with a shading of contempt, and tends to create a caricature. (Arce, 66)

"Ritmo gordo" (literally "fat rhythm") may indeed evoke "greasy bodies," but the image also foregrounds the density and depth of the sound of the word "gordo": the "ritmo" is what is being described as "gordo" not the bodies. An ungreased body can dance to a "ritmo gordo." This focus on the rhythm must be underscored because "Danza Negra" is one of numerous poems whose subject is a form of dance: the *bomba* in "bombo," the "rumba, macumba, candombe, bámbula" in "Majestad Negra," and the titular dance in "Candombe" are examples (to be treated in detail in this study). The predominance of sonorous o's in "ritmo gordo" is only one of several devices Palés uses to evoke a dense medium, the concretization of the timeless state in which the poem takes place:

> Es la raza negra que ondulando va
> En el ritmo gordo del mariyandá.
>
> [It's the black race swaying wave on wave
> In the corpulent rhythm of mariyandá.]

As these lines state, it is through the medium of the dense rhythm that the black soul weaves. To prove this point, we can compare this occurrence of the "medium" device with its function in another line. The same density is evoked by the image "grave son":

> Pasan tierras rojas, islas de betún:
> Haití, Martinica, Congo, Camerún;
> las papiamentosas islas del volcán,
> que en el grave son
> del canto se dan.
>
> [Red lands parade, shoe-blacking islands:
> Haiti, Martinique, Congo, Cameroon;
> papamiento islands of volcano born
> that abandon themselves
> in the chant's grave sound.]

Palés employs "grave son" to syntactically extract from "canto" its soul. Syntactically ambiguous, the "grave son" becomes the medium or state that either evokes the "tierras" and "islas," or is the medium/state in which they (as, in a previous stanza, the "negra" or the "Cocoroco-a) surrender to the "canto," or—as is only possible in a poetic grammar—both possibilities simultaneously.

As with "gordo" (translated as "corpulent" in the poem), Arce lists several connotations of "grave," asserting as well that "more than sonorous gravity" what Palés intended was to evoke "moral gravity." This is highly questionable, especially since the "tierras rojas" and "islas de betún" are also metaphorical dancers. Instead, it would appear that, like "gordo," "grave" is intended to evoke the medium/state in which the poem takes place. Arce's description even inadvertently expresses the identity that Palés establishes between the two words: she describes "grave son" as "a slow and profound rhythm," a phrase employing the adjective "profound," as Palés often does, to suggest depth and density. The difference, of course, is that Palés encapsules his reiteration of that evocation in the image "ritmo gordo." To carry out this proof one step further, we should look at the importance of the dense-medium device in Palés's other poems. A similar invocation of a medium/state is found in "Pueblo Negro." Here, while employing other related devices—to be discussed later in this chapter—the narrator invokes a world that is "amoniacal y denso" ("ammonia-like and dense"). Also, in "Elegía del Duque de la Mermelada" the speaker suggests that the drumbeats are thick drops of night into which the duke would sink:

> Se acabaron tus noches con su suelta cabellera de fogatas
> y su gotear soñoliento y perenne de tamboriles
> en cuyo fondo te ibas hundiendo como un lodo tibio
> hasta llegar a la márgenes últimas de tu gran bisabuelo.

> [Gone are your nights with their flowing hair of bonfire
> and their drowsy, steady dripping like drumbeats,
> into whose depths you'd sink slowly as into warm mud
> to the farthest shores of your great, great grandfather.

The "hundiendo como en un lodo tibio" evokes the same image as "gordo" and "grave," a dense medium, by emphasizing the predominant o-sound. Similarly, the word "soñoliento" evokes the night's density, which, as the poet explicitly informs us, is like "lodo tibio" ("warm mud"). Arce's playing down the literal and phonological dimensions of "gordo" and "grave," to argue that "gordo" was intended to evoke caricature and clumsiness and "grave" with "gravedad moral," is a reading that contradicts Palés's stylistic patterns.

These patterns also show that if, as Arce observed, a contrast does exist between "gordo" and "grave," it is only a surface contrast: the "ritmo gordo" belongs to the dance and the "grave son" belongs to the chant, the former suggesting bodies and the latter voices. But even though one image describes the external (body) and the other the internal (voice), thus provoking the observer/ observed contrast that Arce indicates, in Palés's lexicon "grave" also evokes depth and penetration, alluding to the spiritual, and "gordo" evokes a sense of a penetrable substance (like "allá," "abajo," "lodo," "profundo") typical of these medium-words in which or through which Palés's persona consistently travels to the spiritual state. Besides being two distinct sensorial aspects of the same chant/dance, the density evoked by the meaning and open vowel of "gordo" functions in the poem identically as the depth evoked by the meaning and open vowel of "grave"; the difference is one of focus. Both words function semantically and phonologically as synonyms without the monotony of repetition.

In the end, Arce's analysis fails in the manner of descriptions by linguists who are not critics and who are prone to describe formal linguistic relations in literary texts without indicating whether or how the relations described are important to the writing or reading of the work itself. Arce compounds this failure by never explaining why she chose to study the adjectives and by later concluding that the poem has as many adjectives as verbal forms. She herself noted that ultimately "the adjectives in 'Danza Negra' cannot be studied or evaluated by abstracting them from the line or sentence in which they are inserted like custom-fitted pieces of a mosaic" (Arce, 74). Lastly, except for her references to some aesthetic effect or stylistic device that frequently appears in Palés's poems, her analysis doesn't study Palés's style as a system.

Of her three essays, however, "Tres Pueblos Negros: Algunas Observaciones sobre el Estilo de Luis Palés Matos" ("Three Black Towns: Some Observations on the Style of Luis Palés Matos")[18] does offer a more useful stylistic analysis. This essay compares three writings, all about a "black town": a prose piece titled "Pueblo de Negros" and the poems "Esta Noche He Pasado" and "Pueblo Negro." Of the difference between the prose piece and the earlier poem, "Esta Noche," Arce concludes that the former was really a prose draft of the latter, and both are reactions of Palés's walk through a black sector of his town ("Tres Pueblos" 177). the third poem, "Pueblo Negro" recreates an "imaginary reality, evoked, distant, a product perhaps of literary recollections, a dreamed and desired reality . . ." (177). According to

Arce, "Pueblo Negro," reflecting Palés's mature style, is an expression of a desire to escape the tedium of modernity to an idealized primitive state, to be maliciously playful to the point of scandalizing the bourgeoisie, by juxtaposing refinement and grossness, by mixing "the dream and a delight in the unpleasant and the sexual" ("Tres Pueblos Negros" 186), offering as an illustration of the unpleasant and sexual mix this stanza from "Pueblo Negro":

> El hipopótamo compacto se hunde
> en su caldo de lodo suculento,
> y el elefante de marfil y grasa
> rumia bajo el baobab su vago sueño.
>
> [The compact hippo submerges
> in a succulent mud broth,
> and the fat and ivory elephant
> chews his vague dream under the baobab.]

As well, this mixture contributes to the creating of an atmosphere, which Arce also ascribes to Palés's concentrating on imagery that heightens our awareness of the senses ("Tres Pueblos Negros," 186).

Unfortunately, consistent with Arce's tone throughout, her article ends on an arrogantly Westernist, racist note, celebrating the myth of the superiority of the rational, beauty-aspiring European over the sensual, physical *"tropical"*:

> Like all "tropicals," Palés frequently loses his sense of moderation and lapses into exuberance, intemperance, or the shrill, into a fascination with vulgarity; but he redeems himself from these falls by his skillfull use of language, his intimate aspiration for beauty. . . . ("Tres Pueblos Negros," 187)

Moreover her final critique confirms a suspicion that, deep down, Arce read Palés unsympathetically, respecting his technical skills without taking him seriously enough to attempt to understand his untraditional discourse. Not merely intending to scandalize the bourgeois, Palés's style affirms that in nature Arce's terms "refinement" and "grossness" are meaningless. Only in a narrow class and social context do they acquire meaning and become the stuff of convention—conventions, both linguistic and social, that Arce was incapable of seeing beyond and that Palés quite obviously disavowed.

If one adheres to Arce's interpretation, "Pueblo Negro" be-

comes a roguish fantasy describing with colorful linguistic pyro-
technics the sexual atmosphere that permeates an imaginary,
prototypically black town. But "Pueblo Negro" is less about
"dreamed things," which it obviously does comprise, than about
the act of dreaming a black town:

> Esta noche me obsede la remota
> visión de un pueblo negro
>
> [Tonight I keep seeing in the distance
> a vision of a black town]

The poem is about a voyage taken by means of mimetic graphic
images and evocative sounds. Guided by the persona, who keeps
us aware of his unconsciousness by interrupting the dream so
we may contrast it with reality, we travel with him: "Allá entre
las palmeras" ["Far-off among the palms"] where "está tendido
el pueblo. . . ." ["the town is spread out. . ."]. Although the poet
writes as if the vision had made him think of the town's names,
stylistic patterns argue the contrary. This black town was probably
unconsciously inspired, as was "Kalahari," by his having been
obsessed with the names of African towns. The doorways to the
evoked town de "sueño" are the proper names of the real towns,
"Mussumba, Tombuctú, Farafangana." Thus, the incantation of
the names before the speaker returns to his dream:

> —Mussumba, Tombuctú, Farafangana—
> es un pueblo de sueño,
> tumbado allá en mis brumas interiores
> a la sombra de claros cocoteros.
>
> . . . .
> Allá entre las palmeras
> está tendido el pueblo . . .
> —Mussumba, Tombuctú, Farafangana—
> Caserío irreal de paz y sueño.
>
> [—Mussumba, Timbucktu, Farafangana—
> a town of dream
> flung far-off in my misty soul
> in the shade of clear coconut groves
>
> . . . .
> Far-off among the palm trees
> the town lies before me . . .
> —Mussumba, Timbucktu, Farafangana—
> Unreal houses of peace and dream.]

The names of two of those towns share with the song in the air the same predominant vowel: "ú." The song also has "guturaciones alargadas" (prolonged gutturals") like those in another pair of town names (-uctú-, -angana-), sounds that evoke the images that eventually become the poem.

Once the town is evoked, we discover that its idyllic natural setting is in an atmosphere filled with the sensual song of "la negra," whom the poem depicts as singing "un canto monorrítmico":

> Alguien disuelve perezosamente
> un canto monorrítmico en el viento,
> pululado de úes que se aquietan
> en balsas de diptongos soñolientos,
> y de guturaciones alargadas
> que dan un don de lejanía al verso.
>
> Es la negra que canta
> su sobria vida de animal doméstico;
> le negra de las zonas soleadas
> que huele a tierra, a salvajina, a sexo.
> es la negra que canta,
> y su canto sensual se va extendiendo
> como una clara atmósfera de dicha
> bajo la sombra de los cocoteros.
>
> [Someone lazily dissolves in the wind
> a monorhythmic song
> swarming with *u*-sounds quelled
> on rafts of dreamslow diphthongs
> and prolonged gutturals
> that lend the charm of distance to the line.
>
> It is the black woman singing
> her sober life of a domestic animal;
> the black woman from sunbaked zones,
> who smells of earth, of game, of sex.
> It is the black woman singing,
> and her sensual song spreads without bound
> like a sheer atmosphere of bliss
> in the shade of the palm trees.]

Her song is "monorrítmico," which at once signifies a refrained rhythm but can also be an example of Palés's questionable racist punning, as the word can be read facetiously as "having the rhythm of a monkey." This reading would subvert the poem and is really unnecessary, and yet it is difficult to read Palés stylistic patterns and overlook that Palés would not have let that pun stand without at least being aware of its existence. Equally offensive to a contemporary consciousness, the woman's life is of a "domestic animal," who sings as if preparing a recipe, dissolving her song in the air.

But those lines also suggest something else. The "canto" the woman "disuelve" is a popularly/nuanced pun, also signifying her sex and by extension her source, her core. Moreover, as the first line ends abruptly at the adverb, suggesting a closure, and disregarding the need for a reflexive (a straining for pun characteristic of Palés, as is borne out in several examples), the line suggests an intransitive sense for "disuelve" (helped by the second line's "en el viento") reinforcing the image that in dissolving her "canto" the woman herself is dissolving "en el viento." This intention is stylistically confirmed by Palés consistent pattern of women images as a constant change of physical states, as treated in detail in chapter 7. But this reading is further substantiated in the subsequent stanzas of "Pueblo Negro," in which both meanings rise to the surface structure:

> 1)
> Es la negra que canta
> su sobria vida de animal doméstico;
>
> [It is the black woman who sings
> her sober life of a domestic animal . . .]
>
> 2)
> Es la negra que canta
> y su canto sensual se va extendiendo
>
> [It is the black woman singing,
> and her sensual song spreads without bound . . .]

In the above example 1) the verb *cantar* is followed by the direct object "vida," which is made a metaphor of a song. Thus the implicit song being sung is also a metaphor of her existence. In example 2), her "sobria vida" and her "canto" fuse into one image, "canto," so when her "canto sensual se va extendiendo" we understand that it is her presence, her being.

Ultimately, Palés is telling us that the "canto sensual" coming from her throat is the same sensual force that emanates from the rest of her body redolent "a tierra, a selvajina, a sexo." When the dream ends, and the town and the woman are gone, what remains in his awaking soul is the "ú" sound, the "ú profunda del diptongo fiero," the "ú" now a figurative uterus, rising out of his language and soul from the same source: that black woman's "canto." His Caribbean soul, then, is defined, inspirited, inspired and made fecund by its harboring in his language that African procreative woman/sex/song:

> Al rumor de su canto
> todo se va extinguiendo,
> y sólo queda en mi alma
> la ú profunda del diptongo fiero,
> en cuya curva maternal se esconde
> la armonía prolífica del sexo.
>
> [As her song shrinks to a murmur
> everything begins to fade,
> till the only thing in my soul
> is the fierce diphthong's bass *u*
> whose maternal curvature secretes
> the prolific harmony of sex.]

This poem of the unconscious represents, as Arce herself has indicated, a final stage of three writings on black towns. But the differences between "Pueblo Negro" and the other two writings tells us more than Arce reveals in her description. In "Pueblo Negro," Palés internalizes what in the other two he had merely observed; a town of dreamstuff, the final "Pueblo Negro," exists eternally in his language and collective unconscious. Thus, as in numerous other poems, Palés perceives in his soul the sensuality he believes to be peculiarly African and Caribbean. In this poem, in a night setting, he envisions a mythological explanation of the source of that sexuality. This is a far cry from merely seeking "exuberance" or a "delight in vulgarity," as Arce explained. Palés may be accused of sexually stereotyping the African component of Caribbean culture by centering so many of his poems on sexual imagery, but—and here is the contradiction after images like "monorítmico" and "animal doméstico"—his internalizing that imagery into his own soul makes plain that we are not dealing with a racist satirist of African culture. Sexuality, according to Palés, is good and he clearly believed that his un-Victorian feelings are the result of his un-European lineage.

Owing to the notable absence of substantive critical investigation to this contradictory, highly complex poet, I offer this study, whose focus is to arrive at a better understanding of Luis Palés Matos's themes through an analysis of his style. A selection has been made of those poems that best provide the evidence for this analysis. Conventionally, Palés's "complete" work has been split by critics into two components, white and black poems. This analysis will dispense that separation, which really makes no sense. Except for the cultural theme and imagery in the Afro-Antillean poems, Palés does nothing different in them than what he succeeds in doing with the supposedly "white" poems. Their relation to each other is chronological, with the Afro-Antillean poems concomittant with *Canciones de la vida media*, marking his poetic maturity.

One of the signs of Palés's mature style is his focus on language as his subject. Critics at some point also allude to his intuitive phonological sense, but beyond onomatopoeia relatively little critical analysis is devoted to Palés's linguistic consciousness and its role in his poetry. As observed earlier, Palés underscores the importance of language as a theme by opening *Tuntún* with "Preludio en Boricua." Tomás Blanco was right in telling us that Palés wrote Afro-Antillean poetry to project a Jungian vision of a collective Puerto Rican (and Caribbean) unconscious, but that was also another way of saying that Palés arrived at that vision by means of his culture's spoken language, a linguistic consciousness that, toward different effects, had operated in his poems before *Tuntún*.

Palés's first expression of interest in language as theme and subject was his coauthoring, with José I. de Diego Padró, "Orquestación Diepálica," a poem whose single device, despite appearances of *jitanjáfora*, was onomatopoetic images of night sounds:

> ¡Guau ¡Guau Au-au, au-au, huuummm . . .
> La noche. La luna. El campo . . . huuummm . . .
> Zi, zi, zi-zi, zi-zi, co-quí, co-quí, co-quí . . .
> Hierve la abstrusa zoología en la sombra.
> ¡Silencio Huuuuuummmmmm . . .[19]

This one-poem experiment, "Diepalismo," (from the first syllables of each poet's paternal surname) lacked serious aspirations other than to comment on the prevalent poetry of the time. In a footnote that accompanied the poem, the poets explained their minimalist intentions to make one word "embody in light forms and elements of expression the most solid architectural ideal, suppressing that voluminous symphonic mechanism . . . that today drowns modern poetry with its melodramatic petulance" (De Diego Padró, 30).

Years later, in an interview, Palés defined that literary adventure thusly:

> The aesthetic of *diepalismo* (as the experiment was christened) converted the poetic art into a kind of X-ray enlarger. Anecdotal elements were done away with, and we went directly to the creation of an art of sounds, articulation and murmurs, extracting all plastic possibilities.[20]

It is this desired plasticity that accounts for the frequent use of both the onomatopoetic and more subtle phonological devices, such as the dependence on the pure sound of "gordo" and "grave" and "ú" to evoke a medium.

Unfortunately, Palés's critics, as if all his poems were minimalist orquestrations of *diepalismo,* have limited their treatments of his linguistic consciousness to surface sounds, disregarding or unaware that the Palesian persona is ever exploring the deeper semantic level that gives meaning to those sounds. Within five years of the publication of "Orquestación Diepálica," for example, Palés wrote "Canción de la Vida Media" ("Mid-life Song," the titular poem of an unpublished book), in which he announced his coming of age as a poet, of discovering the more important deeper level of both a poem and life. This intentionally ambiguous poem opens with a statement of the poet's Verlainean intention to "cantar sin palabras":

> Ahora vamos de nuevo a cantar alma mía;
> a cantar sin palabras.
>
> [Now we are going to sing again, my soul,
> sing without words.]

The desire to sing without words reiterates the same minimalist notion expressed in his description of "Orquestación Diepálica." Also, again echoing that description, the following two lines differentiate between surface rhetorical imagery and true poetry:

> Desnúdate de imágenes y poda extensamente
> tus viñas de hojarasca.
>
> [Undress yourself of images and thoroughly prune
> your vineyards of dead leaves.]

Only after the "viñas" are properly pruned will the essence or the fruit ripen fully.

In the third stanza, the poet speaks simultaneously of his literary and biographical infancy, noting that his soul should now avoid "las retóricas travesuras ingenuas":

> Anda el viejo camino para que se te vea
> la intención noble y clara,
> y huye de las retóricas travesuras ingenuas
> que inquietaron tu infancia.

> [Walk the old road so others can see
> the noble and clear design,
> and avoid the ingenuous rhetorical pranks
> that distressed your start.]

He then imagines his maturity, both poetic and emotional, as a fruit clinging from the highest branch, and in an obvious reference to the difference between sensorial surface and deeper meaning, reiterates that so the tree's life-force will cause the fruit to ripen the excess foliage had to fall:

> Ya eres vieja, alma mía, Arbol que entra
> en la zona de la vida media.
> Como fruta madura te cuelga el sentimiento
> de la rama más alta.

> Rama de bella fronda que perfumó mi canto,
> ahora se ve pelada . . .
> Para cuajar el fruto tuvieron que caerse
> las hojas de la rama.

> [You are old now, my soul, Tree that enters
> the zone of middle life.
> Like ripened fruit your perceptions hang
> from the highest branch.

> The beautifully foliaged branch that perfumed my song
> is now bald . . .
> So the fruit may flesh,
> all its leaves had to fall.]

As discussed earlier, twelve years later the metaphor of a well-pruned, fruit-bearing tree served as the unifying metaphor of *Tuntún de Pasa y Grifería*: "Tronco," "Rama," "Flor." This metaphor is not coincidental; Palés began writing his Afro-Antillean poems at the time that he was still working on poems from the unpublished *Canciones de la Vida Media* (c. 1925) and this collection contains his poems most similar in structure and style to those in *Tuntún*. In other words, as the poem "Canción de la Vida Media" shows, with Palés's maturity came his growing cognizance of language's deeper levels. One aspect of this linguistic consciousness is his sense of language as a terrain of time. Palés obsessively explores this dual theme, language as time and a figurative space, to some degree in all poems. Structured like three dimensional maps, his poems record the path of his passage through time/ language while he is transported inward, up and across, always to the same distant metaphysical destination.

3

Topography of Passage and Encounter

Around 1920, Luis Palés Matos wrote the following group of poems:

"Los Animales Interiores" ("The Interior Animals")
"Voces del Mar" ("Sea Voices")
"Voz de lo Sedentario y Monótono" ("Voice of the Sedentary and Monotonous")
"Las Torres Blancas" ("The White Towers")
"El Sueño" ("The Dream")
"El Destierro Voluntario" ("The Voluntario Exile")
"Y una Mano Extraña" ("And a Strange Hand")
"Elegía del Saltimbanqui" ("Elegy of the Acrobat")
"Este Olor a Brea" ("This Smell of Tar")
"Los Funerales de Amor" ("The Funerals of Love")
"Abajo" ("Below")
"Orquestación Diepálica" (*Diepalica* Orquestration")
"Dilema" ("Dilemma")
"Karedín Barbarroja" ("Karedín Redbeard")
"A un Amigo" ("To a Friend")

Not part of any book, this stylistically diverse assortment suggests that during the period of their writing Palés was as yet trying to find a particular style. "Abajo," a celebration of modernity, including mechanized modernity, stands alone among his more characteristic celebrations of the immaterial; "Orquestación Diepálica," besides illustrating Palés's fascination with sounds, remained a one-poem experiment; and "Voz de lo Sedentario y lo Monótono," is a remnant—and actually composed—of earlier poems on the vacuity of small town life. But some of the listed poems prefigure later mature poems in different and important ways. "Este Olor a Brea," for example, is the obvious model for "Canción de Mar" just as "Elegía del Saltimbanqui" strongly resembles "Elegía del Duque de la Mermelada." Still, the most im-

59

portant poems of this group, "Los Animales Interiores," "Las Torres Blancas," and "El Sueño" signal a turn to that feature of the Palesian style which will become a hallmark of his major poems from *Canciones de la Vida Media* to the Filí-Melé cycle: a structure evoking a sense of distance and passage.

In "Los Animales Interiores," for instance, the reader enters the speaker's soul portrayed as a far, rainy place in which an old horse (a surreal, Jungian self-portrait) stands in the rain. Reality in this poem is divided into mundane reality and an inner, spiritual or soul-world in which we experience an altered sense of physics:

> Ese caballo está dentro de mí, ese viejo
> caballo que la lluvia—mustio violín—alarga,
> igual que sobre un lienzo crepuscular lo miro
> proyectarse hacia el vago fondo de mi nostalgia.
>
> Todo tiene una exangüe repercusión interna,
> que la lluvia con blandos bemoles acompaña,
> y me veo un caballo fantasmal y remoto
> allá en una pluviosa lejanía de alma.
>
> [That horse is inside me, that old
> horse that the rain—sorrowful violin—elongates,
> as if on a twilight canvas I watch it
> stretch toward the vague floor of my yearning.
>
> Everything emits a bloodless internal repercussion
> the raindrops accompany with soft flats,
> and I see myself as a horse, phantasmal and far,
> away in a rainy expanse of soul.]

"Las Torres Blancas" describes the soul as the site of a dream city to which the speaker flies when he dreams:

> Sueño, bajo la comba de la noche estrellada
> con una ciudad llena de graves torres blancas.
>
> [I dream, under the starry night's vault,
> a city entirely of solemn, white towers.]

After recreating the city, the poem returns the reader to mundane reality in the final four lines, which evoke a sense of distance between mundane reality and the reality of the dream city:

> Yo anhelo, en el silencio de la noche estrellada,
> cuando las pesadillas de escarbajos bajan

a roerme los sueños, tender mis fuertes alas
hacia la ciudad lúcida de graves torres blancas.

[I want, in the starry night's silence,
when black beetle nightmares descend
to gnaw at my dreams, to spread my powerful wings
toward the radiant city of solemn, white towers.]

Similarly, in "El Sueño" true reality is depicted as an infinite ocean of dream in whose depths ephemeral, mundane reality is only an insignificant turbulence:

El sueño es el estado natural. Nuestras vidas
sólo turban con leves, fugaces movimientos,
ese ras de agua inmóvil perennemente mudo,
muy allá de los límites del espacio y el tempo.

Nuestra acción se disuelve como una vaga onda.
Todo fina en la oculta voluntad del silencio
cuya oleosa esencia de mutismo circula
por el vasto engranaje vital del universo.

[Dreaming is the natural state. Our lives
only disrupt with mild, fleeting ripples
that flat water surface, perennially mute,
far beyond the borders of space and time.

Our every act dissolves like an uncresting wave.
Everything ends in the secret will of the silence
whose oily, mute essence lubricates
the enormous gears of the universe.]

In other poems of that early group, the distance structure operates more subtly. The same "lejano país," the imagination or the soul, now rendered in geographic images, haunts the man in the wheelchair in "Voz de lo Sedentario y lo Monótono." In the face of "Días iguales—largos como caras sobrías" ["Identical days—long like somber faces"], the speaker, confined to a wheelchair, dreams of emigrating. Among his ruminations, the speaker creates an image of a dividing line between his anxious soul and his body trapped in a small town:

La carne, ese fermento de manzana podrida.
La soledad absorbe como esponja vacía,
y abajo, un gusaneo de miseria, y arriba . . .

[The flesh, that rotten-apple ferment.
The solitude absorbs like a dry sponge,
and below, a worming misery, and above . . .]

Further on, he reiterates his desire to travel vicariously, this
tie placing emphasis on the means of arriving at his vision of a
far place:

Iría así, de viaje, por un camino interminable, en un cupé largo, pesado y gris.
Y jadear el cansancio del caballo y tener
la remota visión de un lejano país.

[I'd go on like this, touring, along an interminable road, in a long landau, heavy and gray.
And panting like a tired horse and harboring
the remote vision of a country far away.]

A sense of demarcation between the *here* and *over there*, as well
as the stress on the journey and more than on the actual destination, is also present in "A un Amigo." Here the "reposar/larga-
mente" ("resting long") that appears in the first stanza becomes,
in the fourth and fifth stanzas, a passage in a dream state:

¡Feliz tú que te fuiste a la oportuna hora
en que todo lo invade la nostalgia del gris,
por ese mar callado sin noche y sin aurora
con rumbo hacia un ignoto y lejano país!

Duerme tu inalterable sueño, tú que reposas
largamente en la paz del ataúd, . . .

[Happy you who departed at the perfect hour,
when the gray's nostalgia saturates thoroughly
across that mute sea without night or daybreak,
with a tide toward an unknown, far away country!

Sleep your unchanging dream, you who reposes
long in the quiet of the casket, . . .]

A proper reading of these early poems requires that we identify
a semantic structure that evokes a sense of distance. But, as is
evident from the examples presented, more than a sense of distance, this structure engages our reading in a sense of both transit
to and relocation in another state of mind or site of action. Once
there, the poet has an encounter with an image of a spiritual

force, a god, or a "numen." The underlying structure, then, is of passage and encounter, whether or not this structure is readily decipherable from the surface text. In "Los Animales Interiores," we encounter the soul-world immediately, semantically assuming a passage to it. In "Las Torres Blancas," we are first thrust into the dream; at the end, the speaker makes a surface reference to arriving there by means of a metaphorical flight. In "Voz de lo Sedentario y lo Monótono" and "El Sueño," the surface text expressly refers to traveling to "un lejano país." These poems serve as models for appreciating the dreamed distant lands in "Los Funerales de Amor" and "Karedín Barbarroja," poems also intended to transport us to far, imagined destinations.

Another variation on the passage structure operates in "Este Olor a Brea" in which the odor of tar transports the speaker back to the port of his small town. The actual portrayal of the town is, at this point, less germane than that an evocation takes the speaker from one place to another. This leap is textually encoded by the ellipsis, signifying the deletion of any intermediary steps, which follow the refrain:

> Este olor a brea me trae el puerto . . .

> [This smell of tar delivers the port . . .]

Besides being a voyage to his home town, the poem also returns him to an evoked town in another time, the town as the speaker remembers it.

This matrix also structures a poem that prefigures more mature poems, "Elegí del Saltimbanqui" ["Elegy of the Acrobat"], a poem of shifting verbal tenses, evoking a chronological trajectory of a decline, in this case of the acrobat. The poem opens in the perfective past and moves to the imperfective past, to the present, finally the future:

1. ¡Oh flaco saltimbanqui del circo de la aldea!
2. Se acabó tu alegría, terminó tu cabriola.
3. Se ha descubierto el fácil resorte de tus trucos
4. cuando en el escenario desatas tus maromas.

5. Ya no asustas a nadie cuando repites esa
6. caída espeluznante del trapecio a la argolla,
7. ni cuando sobre el filo del espadón brillante
8. como un flexible elástico de nervios te desgonzas.

9. Has perdido la gracia que improvisara antaño
10. fantásticos deslices, absurdas maniobras;
11. a fuer de repetirte te has vuelto monorrítmico
12. y es arte del pasado tu muscular retórica.

13. Los niños en la calle ya dominan tu ciencia,
14. y hasta del payaso lento y rollizo mejora
15. el salto de la muerte con que antaño solías
16. deleitar a la ingenua congregación absorta.

[1. Oh skinny, small-town circus acrobat!
2. Your fun is over, your caper is up.
3. Everyone sees through the easy ruse
4. when you perform your stunts on stage.

5. Now you startle none when you repeat
6. that hair-raising fall from the ring trapeze,
7. nor when, against the glistening broadsword's edge,
8. like a supple elastic of nerves, you cut yourself in half.

9. Lost is the grace that once could improvise
10. fantastic slides, bizarre maneuvers;
11. having to repeat them has made you predictable
12. and your muscular rhetoric is art of the past.

13. Children in streets now know your technique,
14. and even the slow, roly-poly clown improves upon
15. your leap of death that in yesteryears
16. thrilled the ingenuous, riveted audience.]

On a semantic level, lines 1–8 announce the decline of the "saltimbanqui" whose old stunts no longer amaze and (9–14) take us back to when he (Palés, the *modernista* poet? Perhaps Darío?) entertained (15–16) with rhetorical tricks. In the perfective past, these lines flow into those in the imperfective past of the "antaño" (the farthest *time when*). Notice the change in tense starting with line 17:

17. Contra la carpa blanca del circo, tu figura,
18. es hoy una andrajienta caricatura estólida,
19. cuando chupado de hambre pasas meditabundo
20. igual que un espantajo de miseria y de sombra.

21. Has caído en desgracia, maromero de circo.
22. El público, cansado, te exige nuevas formas
23. y tú estás ya muy viejo para ensayar argucias
24. que te den el sentido de las últimas modas.

25. Un día, cualquier día, de un salto desgraciado,
26. rodarás por el suelo con la cabeza roja,
27. y esa maroma trágica, desconcertante y muda,
28. será tu más notable y aplaudida maroma.

[17. Against the pale circus tent, your figure
18. is now a ragged, ridiculous parody
19. when sucked-in starving you pass by abstracted
20. like a scarecrow of misery and shadow.

21. You've fallen into ruin, circus rope walker.
22. The bored public demands new techniques
23. and you're too old now to learn tricks
24. that would make you appear up to date

25. One day, any day, from an ill-fated leap,
26. you'll roll on the ground with your head split open,
27. and that tragic stunt, distressing and speechless,
28. will be your most memorable and applauded stunt.

Lines 17–20 consist of sentences in the present tense. Lines 21–24 return to the perfective for the duration of one line (27) to introduce a stanza in the present and thereby draw a hard edge contrasting the past and present life of the "saltimbanqui." The final stanza, a second ending, takes us beyond the present to a vision of the final "maroma" ("stunt").

In the unpublished *Canciones de la Vida Media (Midlife Songs)* (1925), the passage structure undergoes a major semantic shift: whereas the just-discussed transitional poems focused on the object of encounter (such as the horse and the dream city), poems in *Canciones* evoke the passage or medium through which we are transported. Compare the titles "Los Animales Interiores" and "Las Torres Blancas" from the 1920 poems to those in from *Canciones*, "El Pozo" ("The Well") or "Topografía" ("Topography"). The former pair of titles call attention to things found in the dream or soul while the latter pair evokes the medium of the entire experience, the *interioridad* as opposed to the *animales* of these poems. "El Pozo" is one of the most sophisticated examples of this shift:

Mi alma es como un pozo de agua sorda y profunda
en cuya paz solemne e imperturbable ruedan
los días, apagando sus rumores mundanos
en la quietud que cuajan las oquedades muertas.

[My soul is like a well of deaf, deep water
on whose solemn, imperturbable peace
the days circle, extinguishing worldly murmurs
in the quiet that dead hollows curdle.]

In this stanza several semantic operations take place not immediately evident in the surface text. For even though we understand that "pozo" is "un pozo de agua" and that the subsequent lines modify "pozo," on a surface level those modifiers, like "sorda y profunda," specifically modify "agua." The surface-semantic integrity of "pozo de agua" is sustained by our assuming the term denotes one whole thing and by the poem's exploiting the ambiguities of "en," which means both "in" and "on." This ambiguity carries over to the second stanza in which "pozo" is separated from "agua":

Abajo el agua pone su claror de agonía:
irisación morbosa que en las sombras fermenta;
linfas que se coagulan en largos limos negros
y exhalan esta exangüe y azul fosforescencia.

[Below, the water lays its scream-bright clarity:
a gloomy iridescence that ferments in the shadows;
lymphs that coagulate in long black slime
and exhale this bloodless, blue phosphorescence.]

Opening with the prominant adverb "Abajo," the line stresses the depth of the "agua," in whose murky substance appear the images of the stanza's subsequent lines. Returning the reader to the surface, the following line reintroduces the word "pozo," evoking an image of the pool as a whole, like the surface of a mirror:

Mi alma es como un pozo. El paisaje dormido
turbiamente en el agua se forma y se dispersa,
y abajo, en lo más hondo, hace tal vez mil años,
una rana misántropa y agazapada sueña.

[My soul is like a well. The sleepy landscape
in the water turbulently gathers and disperses,
and below, at its deepest, maybe a thousand years back
a clinging, misanthropic frog is dreaming.]

The ambiguous "en," as it did in the first stanza, connects the image of the water's surface (evoked by "pozo") to the "agua," which by now signifies the depths into which the poem descends once more. But this time to a depth so deep that the descent becomes a passage back in time. Here the descent ends, although not the poem, which continues to develop the distance/time device in a closing stanza that summarizes the poem's entire trajectory:

> A veces al influjo lejano de la luna
> el pozo adquiere un vago prestigio de leyenda;
> se oye el cró-cró profundo de la rana en el agua,
> y un remoto sentido de eternidad lo llena.

> [At times under the moon's far-off spell,
> the well assumes the misty magic of a fable;
> a frog's deep croaking echoes in its water,
> and it fills with a remote sense of eternity.]

The moon's presence adds another dimension to the mundane setting, opening the immediate site to infinity (a concept of both distance and time). Down from space, the moon's light falls on the visually whole image of the "pozo" (as opposed to the "agua"), and affected by that light, in the water's depths, "en lo más profundo, hace tal vez mil años" ["at its deepest, maybe a thousand years back"], the previously mentioned frog is croaking, a prehistoric sound from its prehistoric depths. The elements that had been separated by the surface text are reunited: the croaking is heard "en el agua" yet what is filled with "un remoto sentido de eternidad" is the "lo" of the "pozo," thus infusing the mundane with spirituality.

The dualism of the surface "pozo" and the deep "agua" typifies only one of the geometric configurations of the passage structure. For, in the Palesian poem, the physical world is depicted as a composite of physical and metaphysical or spiritual properties and the being of a physical thing flows from and is synonymous with its metaphysical or spiritual, unseen other side. This dualism's halves become the contiguous regions of the Palesian topography or geographic medium. Together they constitute the points of origin, destination and return, with the mundane realm as the point of departure and the infinite as the ultimate destination. But that infinity is not "out there" to be reached: reality is submerged in it and seeped with it. The infinite is both destination and medium to the farthest limits of itself, or to use Palés's imagery, with a sponge one possesses the essence of the sea. The eternity in our inner selves, then, when tapped into, is the medium through, across, and into which the speaker and reader travel from the mundane to a distant destination beyond the mundane.

In poems like "El Pozo," with an exterior/interior configuration, the structure pivots on a dividing line between the (physically and spiritually) flat surface and a deep, penetrable medium, although in that poem the line remains without an explicit image in the surface text. A *graphic* expression of that line, however, is found in "Topografía," in which the land around and under the speaker is portrayed as only the surface of something very much a product of its depths. On the surface we see the mundane world, barren and lifeless:

> Esta es la tierra estéril y madrastra
> en donde brota el cacto.

> [This is the sterile, step-mother land
> where what sprouts is cactus.]

Only the dense night opens another dimension: out of its "lugubre / silencio" ["lugubrious silence," as in "Pueblo Negro," Palés associates the stressed "u" with depth], "rompe el sapo / su grito de agua oculta" ["the frog begins / his call like a hidden water"], which "las sombras / absorben como tragos" ["the shadows gulp like drinks"]. Otherwise, everything is

> bajo la línea muerta que recorta
> el ras rígido y firme de los campos.

> [. . . smothered under the dead line that cuts
> the countryside's hard, angular skyline.]

In contrast, the swamp emits the stench of something decomposed, which at night is seen as the ghostly "fuego fatuo":

> Cunde un tufo malsano
> de cosa descompuesta en la marisma
> por el fuego que baja de lo alto;
> fermento tenebroso que en la noche
> arroja el fuego fatuo,
> y da esas largas formas fantasmales
> que se arrastran sin ruido sobre el páramo.

[Everywhere a sickening stench
of something in the marsh decomposed
by the fire from above;
a gloomy ferment that at night
sprouts the will-o-the-wisp
and blooms those long phantasmal forms
that shuffle soundlessly over the plain.]

The final stanza fuses the mundane surface with the subsoil to form a composite image of the speaker's complete history:

Esta es toda mi historia:
sal, aridez, cansancio,
una vaga tristeza indefinible,
una inmóvil fijeza de pantano,
y un grito, allá en el fondo,
como un hongo terrible y obstinado,
cuajándose entre fofas carnaciones
de inútiles deseos apagados.

[This is my entire history:
salt, dryness, fatigue,
a vague, indefinable sadness,
an unrippled, swamp constancy
and a scream, deepest down,
like a monstrous, unstoppable mushroom
curdling among the spongy flesh
of useless aborted desires.]

A third example of this explicit line is found in "Pueblo," a poem similar to "Topografía" in tone and subject matter, but that like "El Pozo" lacks an explicit reference to a dividing line. "Pueblo," in fact, at first glance appears to be unrelated to the passage structure and simply a description of the zero of small town existence. Nevertheless, the passage structure is there, evoked by a subtle geometric design. In the first half the persona summarizes the town's tedium in descriptions whose verbs evoke horizontality:

¡Piedad, Señor, piedad para mi pobre pueblo
donde mi pobre gente se morirá de nada.
Aquel viejo notario que *se pasa* los días
en su mínima y lenta preocupación de rata;
este alcalde adiposo de grande abdomen vacuo
chapoteando en su vida tal como en una salsa;

aquel comercio lento, igual, de hace diez siglos;
estas cabras que *triscan* al resol de la plaza;
algún mendigo, algún caballo que *atraviesa*
tiñoso, gris y flaco, por estas calles anchas;
la fría y atrofiante modorra del domingo
jugando en los casinos *con billar y barajas*;
todo, todo el rebaño tedioso de estas vidas
en este pueblo viejo donde no ocurre nada,
todo esto *se muere, se cae, se desmorona*,
a fuerza de ser cómodo y de estar a sus anchas.

[Pity, Lord, have pity on my poor town
where my poor people will likely die of nothing.
That old notary who *passes* the days
steeped in slow, nibbling rodent's worries;
this greasy mayor with a huge hollow stomach
dabbling in his life as if it were a sauce;
that slow business, unchanged for ten centuries;
those goats *capering* in the plaza's blinding sun;
some beggar, some horse that *crosses*,
scabby, gray and bony, these wide streets;
Sunday's cold, atrophying languor
playing in bars *with pool tables and cards*;
all of it, the whole tedious flock of these lives
in this old town where nothing happens,
all this *dies, falls, collapses*,
from living easy and having everything you need.]
(Italics mine)

The generally horizontal evocations in those lines contrast with
the verbs in the second half, in which he begs God to unleash
an agent who would penetrate, disrupt or act against the town's
flat routine:

¡Piedad, Señor, piedad para mi pobre pueblo.
Sobre estas almas simples, desata algún canalla
que *contra* el agua muerta de sus vidas *arroje*
la piedra redentora de una insólita hazaña . . .
Algún ladrón que *asalte ese Banco en la noche*,
algún Don Juan que *viole esa doncella casta*,
algún tahur de oficio que *se meta en el pueblo*
y *revuelva* estas gentes honorables y mansas.

[Pity, Lord, have pity on my poor town.
Over these simple souls, unleash some rogue
who'd hurl *against* their stagnant-water lives

the liberating stone of a shocking act. . .
Some thief *to break into that Bank in the night,*
some Don Juan *to take that chaste young lady,*
some professional cardshark who would *enter the heart of the town*
and *shuffle* these honorable, sheep-like people.]
(Italics mine)

Clearly, as Palés himself was often transported to some soulful experience by penetrating and thus traveling into himself, he would want his "pueblo" (town/people) to do the same and discover a revitalized essence under their worn out exterior.

The exterior/interior configuration of the three poems discussed might suggest that, as in "El Pozo," the trajectory will always be vertical. In "Humus," however, although the speaker senses "un vaho oscuro de sueño y de cansancio" rising (vertically) from within, the speaker moves horizontally and the interiority referred to is a mundane animal interiority, even if bereft of all aspirations to the sublime because exhausted of the dreamstuff of poetry:

> Sube por mis raíces, del fondo de mí mismo,
> un vaho oscuro de sueño y de cansancio.
> Estoy completamente solo frente a mi abismo . . .
> ¡Qué horror, que aroma rancio!
>
> Detritus de ideales, de pasiones, de anhelos.
> ¡Qué humus triste, qué fuerzas tan serviles
> en las ilusas manos cargadas por los cielos,
> y ahora míseras, viles!
>
> ¡Hasta dónde llegaste, ser mínimo que un día
> creíste claro y límpido el venero!
> Antes, rico estanciero,
> en tus zona azules de poesía,
> y ahora, de tu propia tristeza, pordiosero.

> [Up from my roots, from the core of my self,
> a dark steam of sleep and exhaustion.
> I am completely alone before my abyss . . .
> What a horror, what a rancid smell!
>
> Detritus of ideals, passions, aspirations.
> What a sad humus, what forces once so servile
> in deluded hands carried through the heavens,
> and now wretched, vile!

How far did you get, tiny being who one day
imagined the source clear and clean!
Before a rich rancher,
on your blue acres of poetry,
and now, hungry for your own sorrow, a beggar.]

Accustomed to the lightness of the dream state, his head cannot carry the weight of the mundane world across whose plane he searches for his "gran tristeza":

Buscas tu gran tristeza y encuentras el vacío,
el cansancio del mundo que te pesa
el cual fardo que no puede sostener tu cabeza,
globo lleno de humo, de soledad y hastío.

[You look for your great sorrow and find the void,
the world's weariness that weighs on you
like a bale of goods your head cannot balance,
sphere full of smoke, solitude and loathing.]

This sense of passage in several possible directions operates as well in numerous other poems. A favorite destination in the early poems was the "lejano país." Later, the tree metaphor in "Canción de la Vida Media" telescopes into the subdued metaphor of a prow aimed skyward toward a distant star. This sense of lines crossing the distances between diverse directions eventually expresses itself in a consciousness of a stylistic geometry. The speaker in "Boca Arriba," for instance, lies face up contemplating how the night sky "abre una interrogación," an intentional ambiguity one of whose meanings graphically images the straightening of a question mark into a geometric line:

Estoy boca arriba, al cielo,
que abre una interrogación
geométrica a mi desvelo,
en cada constelación.

[Lying face up, to the sky,
that in every constellation
opens a geometric question
mark to my sleeplessness.]

Another line plumbs from the stars above the hilltops to the speaker who experiences the sensation of dissolving into his contemplation of the infinite night:

Existo, pero no soy
ya en mí, ni seré quizás,
bajo este cielo de hoy
heterogéneo y total.

Abajo, el aturdimiento
de este polvo individual
que vacila, se va al viento,
y no se junta jamás.

Y arriba, la interrogada
mole sin trazo ni rúa;
la Osa Mayor que en la nada
fuerza una extraña ganzúa,

y el pensamiento que viola
la monstruosa pubertad
de la noche y tornasola
de partos la inmensidad . . .

[I exist, but no longer am
in myself, nor perhaps will be
under this today's sky,
absolute and unlike me.

Below, the stupefaction
of this individual dust
that wanders, is blown away,
never again reunited.

And above, the interrogated
massiveness without chart or route;
the Big Dipper that pokes
an odd picklock in the void;

and thoughts that deflower
night's monstrous puberty
until the immensity
dawns with births.]

By outlining the trajectory of the speaker's physical movement
or changes in states of consciousness, Palés directional or line
images chart the medium, another way of saying that the passage
interests the poet as much as the destination. In "Lullaby," the
speaker would appear to travel toward no particular destination.
As in "Humus," here the descent into the interiority intersects
with his movement across the mundane world. The poem opens
with a reference to the mundane world as turning or revolving

while the soul is "aferrada / sobre su tema viejo." That "tema" submerges the soul in the "sueño.":

> ¡Mi pobre alma aferrada,
> sumergida en el sueño
> Mi alma sigue llorando
> sobre su tema viejo.
>
> [My poor bound soul,
> submerged in dream!
> My soul keeps crying
> over its old theme.]

Simultaneously the soul "submerged in the dream" moves across the mundane world, in whose inner core are the caverns:

> Abajo, en las cavernas,
> llenas de tenebrosos aposentos,
> los monstruos del hastío,
> los montruos del hastío están durmiendo . . .
> y ella atraviesa pálida,
> como una larga estela de luceros,
> estas sombras espesas y cuajadas
> de aterrador silencio.
>
> [Below, in the caverns,
> full of shadowy chambers,
> the monsters of boredom
> the monsters of boredom are sleeping . . .
> and, like a long wake of stars,
> it palely glides past them,
> those thick shadows congealed
> from terrifying silence.]

As in "El Pozo," the adverbial expressions of place and distance—*sobre, abajo, allí*—appear in prominant positions to foreground the geometric pattern.

A similar perpendicular pattern is sustained in "Walhalla," a poem that superimposes an imagined Scandinavian setting over that of Palés's hometown, Guayama, a predominantly black town. Here too the speaker moves horizontally across a setting while we are kept cognizant of something *out there*. The activity of this imagined mundane reality takes place as the speaker carries on an interior monologue:

¿Qué buscas; qué persiguen tus cálidos antojos?
¿Qué quiméricas Thules vislumbraron tus ojos?
¿Qué palacio remoto quiere cuajar tu empeño
en los vagos dominios de la bruma y el sueño?

[What do you seek; what do your fevered whims pursue?
What unreal Thules do your eyes glimpse?
What remote palace do you want to materialize
in the vague dominions of the fog and the dream?]

In the next stanza, the exterior and interior worlds intersect as the "burgos negros" pass by and the walker continues his journey:

Pasan los burgos negros en la quietud nocturna,
donde a la tibia atmósfera de crepitantes fuegos,
soñará alguna Svanhild pálida y taciturna
con el rey boreal de los fiordos noruegos.
Pero tú vas impávido, pertinaz y tranquilo . . .
La noche tiende su arco de estrellas a tu anhelo,
pero tú vas impávido, pertinaz y tranquilo,
capitán de las brumas, emperador del hielo.

[The black burghers stroll in the nocturnal quiet,
where in the warm air from a crackling fire
some pale, taciturn Svanhild must dream
of the boreal king of the Norwegian fiords.
But you walk undaunted, determined, relaxed. . .
Night offers its dome of stars to guide you,
but you walk undaunted, determined, relaxed,
captain of the mists, emperor of the ice.]

In *Tuntún de Pasa y Grifería*, the sense of passage through space and time evolves to another stage. Whereas in the majority of the poems already discussed the speaker is transported from the mundane to a remote, timeless place, in *Tuntún* the medium and destination become one, an inspiriting and informing numen to be invoked. Moreover, among the sites of spiritual encounter, history or the past is represented as a mythic realm. "Numen," for example, parallels two mythic passage/invocations that eventually link to form one unbroken trajectory:

Jungla africana—Tembandumba.
Manigua haitiana—Macandal.

[African jungle—Tembandumba.
Haitian thicket—Macandal.]

Tembandumba and Macandal are, of course, numina, informing spiritual principles evoked/invoked when the poet or the "negro" thinks about Africa or Haiti. By this invocation, the synechdochic "negro" dancing the "candombe" in the "jungla" is simultaneously transported to and embodies Tembandumba at the same time that the dancer in "la manigua haitiana" invokes the numen Macandal, who eternally invokes his African numina, including Tembandumba. Like markers on a line of coordinates plotting a trajectory back to eternity, these numinous manifestations coexist in the medium of the timeless dance, in the course of which all "Nigricia" is united. The "candombe" that reunites the "negro" with his numinous origins is also a legacy of the speaker's history and language, which still possesses the word "candombe." Like the "ú profunda" in "Pueblo Negro," "candombe" is a totemic word that contains the images of its past. (This totemic-word device is an example of an important passage device to be treated in greater detail in a later chapter.)

In addition to demonstrating Palés's sense of myth, "Numen" also demonstrates that, except for some rhythmic changes, in *Tuntún* the passage structure that hallmarks Palés's mature style remains unchanged. The "negro" passes from the mundane reality to the superior spiritual reality:

> Atravesando inmensidades
> sobre el candombe su alma va
> al limbo oscuro donde impera
> la negra fórmula esencial.

> [Crossing immense spaces,
> his soul rides the *candombe*
> to the dark limbo that enthrones
> the essential black formula.]

Given the consistency of structural patterns in Palés's poems, it should also not surprise that, certain lexical and syntactic features evident in *Tuntún* are in pre-Afro-Antillean poems. In "Numen," the vertical passage in dance to the "negra fórmula esencial" is the parallel of the horizontal crossing in "Lullaby":

> ¡Ay pobre de mi alma
> que atraviesa estos yermos,
> y que va de puntillas, suavemente,
> para no despertar su propio sueño!
> . . . .

¡Mi alma, mi pobre alma!
Sobre su tema viejo,
atraviesa estos campos, suavemente, . . .

[Ay, my poor soul
that crosses those deserts,
light-hoofed, carefully,
not to awake its own dream!

. . . .
My soul, my poor soul!
mounted on its old theme,
it crosses these fields, carefully, . . .]

("Lullaby")

Another example of parallel passage structures in both an Afro-Antillean and non-Afro-Antillean poem is evident in "Pueblo Negro" and its prefiguration "Las Torres Blancas":

Sueño, bajo la comba de la noche estrellada,
con una ciudad llena de graves torres blancas.

[I dream, under the starry night's vault,
a whole city of solemn, white towers.]

Esta noche me obsede la remota
visión de un pueblo negro . . .

[Tonight I keep seeing in the distance
a vision of a black town . . .]

Situated in an imaginary natural setting, in both poems the "pueblo," the speaker informs us, is "un pueblo de sueño," and the city is a "ciudad de fábula." Except for the specific devices employed to achieve the effect, both are described in a manner that evokes a sense of distance. In "Las Torres Blancas" the city itself is described as "lejana":

Clarores boreales del firmamento bajan,
y en la quietud unánime de la ciudad lejana.

[Northern lights descend from the firmament,
and on the unbroken quiet of the distant city.]

"Pueblo Negro" foregrounds the phonological suggestiveness of the adverbial "allá":

> tumbado allá en mis brumas interiores
> a la sombra de claros cocoteros.
>
> [flung far-off in my misty soul
> in the shade of clear coconut groves.]

In both poems, the natural setting is described as a blurry flora surrounded by a clear air in which there is also fauna:

> Afuera, sobre los campos de pesadilla,
> se alzan arboledas borrosas, y en la atmósfera clara
> se mueve vagamente una exótica fauna
> de monstros sublunares de gelatina diafanas.
>
> [In the outskirts, over nightmare fields,
> rise blurry tree groves, and in the glowing air
> hazily moves an exotic fauna
> of clear gelatin monsters in moonlight.]
>   ("Las Torres Blancas")

> La luz rabiosa cae
> en duros ocres sobre el campo extenso.
> Humean, rojas de calor, las piedras,
> y la humedad del árbol corpulento
> evapora frescuras vegetales
> en el agrio crisol del clima seco.
>
> Pereza y laxitud. Los aguazales
> cuajan un vaho amoniacal y denso.
> El compacto hipopótamo se hunde
> en su caldo de lodo suculento,
> y el elefante de marfil y grasa
> rumia bajo el baobab su vago sueño.
>
> [The furious light hails
> as a cruel ochre over the vast countryside.
> Red-hot, the stones steam,
> and the enormous tree's humidity
> distils a plant coolness
> in the bitter crucible, the dry climate.
>
> Laziness and laxness. The swamps
> curdle an ammonial, dense vapor.
> The compact hippo submerges
> in its succulent mud broth,
> and the fat and ivory elephant
> chews his vague dream under the baobab.]
>   ("Pueblo Negro")

In both distant places, a woman is the sole inhabitant: the "Diosa-Poesía" dwells in the fable city; the black woman resides in a dream town. The black woman, we recall, embodies "canto"; the Diosa-Poesía embodies poetry as her gait beats the rhythm of a poem and her lips "speak falling leaves of prophetic words":

> y la Diosa-Poesía de un cometa escoltada
> va por las alamedas desiertas, cabizbaja.
> Ella es la moradora serena de esta patria . . .
> De su cuerpo desnudo brotan azules llamas
> y sus labios deshojan sibilina palabras.
>
> [and the Goddess-Poetry, guarded by a comet
> walks along the promenade, head bowed.
> She is the serene inhabitant of this fatherland. . .
> blue flames shoot from her nude body,
> and her lips shed oracular words.]

Both poems end by underscoring the poet's ability to return. In "Las Torres Blancas," he suggests by his desire to do so, that when he is haunted by nightmares he would spread wings and fly back to the dream; in "Pueblo Negro," he tells us that the mythic town and the woman-"canto" is ever present in his language, in the deep, womb-shaped *ú*-sound of Spanish.

"Pueblo Negro" also illustrates how the poetry in *Tuntún* conserves some remnants of the passage configuration of the non-Afro-Antillean poems. Despite the shift that differentiates the geographic sense in "Las Torres Blancas" from the sense of linguistic diachrony in "Pueblo Negro," both poems share the same vision of a total reality consisting of an exterior (mundane reality and "ú" sound) distinct from its interior component (dream city and dream town). But also implicit in the geographic configuration of this vision, and really impossible to see from the surface evidence in either poem, is an existential morality of authenticity. According to this morality, there is the surface behavior and the true self that should not be betrayed. This is the sin of inauthenticity. Thus, the interior/exterior configuration also implies an ethical scrutiny, in certain poems of the self alone, in other poems of the self as a social and cultural consciousness.

The themes of authenticity and inauthenticity, then, are semantic structures that parallel the surface structure of passage and encounter. In poems such as "Boca Arriba," "Los Animales Interiores, "Las Torres Blancas," and "Pueblo Negro," Palés encounters his true nature as poet, as citizen of a reality different from the surface world. At other times, in poems such as "Mulata-Antilla," "Kalahari," "Ten Con Ten," he encounters his authentic cultural situation. This kind of cultural or regional or historical encounter predominantly takes place in *Tuntún*, but not consistently: "Topografía" and "Aires Bucaneros" are not part of *Tuntún* and speak for the self as a cultural consciousness; these are also encounters with authenticity. And some examples of this morality theme in *Tuntún* are complicated, or simply obscured, by the poem's also containing imagery that project, or may appear to project, yesteryear's routinely racist perception of blacks.

This implicit morality explains the mixed feelings that are generated in the reader by "Elegía del Duque de la Mermelada." On the one hand, the entire poem seems to insist, solely for racist reasons, that all blacks are savage, even ape-like, and that the Duque more properly belongs in a tribal and natural setting and not in any sophisticated courtly context. Especially offensive are the images of tribal cannibalism ("No longer will you eat the succulent roast child"), or the Duke's inner urge to "'Climb to the cornices of the palace'") or rape his dancing partner. But even when the imagery appears most debasing, when we consider that it was written by a poet who celebrated having regionally or linguistically inherited the spirit of Macandal, Tembandumba, Ogún, the mariyandá, infectious drums, and who ultimately renders homage to those spirits for giving him his cultural identity, this kind of apparent racist imagery can also be a sarcasm on the white man's popular perception of black culture, Palés as a kindred-spirit lampooner. This is patently the case in "Intermedios del Hombre Blanco" ("What Man's Interludes") and "Ñáñigo al Cielo" ("*Ñáñigo* Goes to Heaven"). Moreover, knowing from the evidence of so many poems that Palés feels an identity with his subject, an argument is tenable that his simian allusions are variants on his savage image, and both are really expressions of his own romantic longing for a purer, uncivilized state of being. Nevertheless, that all this argument may sound unconvincing to many readers is wholly understandable; the humor can also appeal to racist tastes. The question to ask, however much the simian imagery complicates the discussion, is whether the focus of ridicule is the (savage/simian) black man or his Frenchification, and we can find an answer to this question in Palés's structural signature: the structure of interiority-exteriority, of authenticity-inauthenticity.

"Elegía" is essentially about a black man donning French clothes and putting on French affectations. Again, is Palés laugh-

ing that a black man should presume to put on the trappings of
civilization or is he chastising that the black man should patheti-
cally dismiss his true self to imitate former French colonizers?
First, we must appreciate that the poem turns the images of African past and French present into symbols of time. We are kept
aware of the difference between the mundane present (French)
and the numinous, inspiriting past (African). A fine line similar
to the one that separated the land surface from the subterranean
essence in "Topografía" divides the poem into the tenses of the
Duque's history. The first stanza rhetorically inquires in the present tense about things that existed in the past:

> ¡Oh mi fino, me melado Duque de la Mermelada.
> ¿Donde están tus caimanes en el lejano aduar del Pongo,
> y la sombra azul y redonda de tus baobabs africanos,
> y tus quince mujeres olorosas a selva y a fango?

> [Oh my fine, my honey-colored Duke of Marmelade!
> Where are your crocodiles in the far-off village on the Pongo,
> and the round blue shadow of your African baobabs,
> and your fifteen wives smelling of mud and the jungle?]

The second stanza employs a *surface* future of "comer," "matar,"
and "rastrear el ojo" to predicate that he will nevermore do any of
those things he used to do, all activities that suggest immersion,
penetration (the giraffe is "effeminate") or ingestion, compared
to the horizontal act of walking around looking courtly:

> Ya no comerás el suculento asado de niño,
> ni el mono familiar, a la siesta, te matará los piojos,
> ni tu ojo dulce rastreará el paso de la jirafa afeminada
> a través del silencio plano y caliente de las sabanas.

> [No longer will you eat the succulent roast child,
> nor will the family monkey kill your lice at siesta,
> nor your fond eye trail the effeminate giraffe
> across the hot flat silence of the plains.]

The first two lines of the next stanza employs the surface perfective past form to contrast with the implied imperfective past
that emerges to the surface in the last two lines, which in turn
ultimately transport us back to the farthest historical point, the
"márgenes últimas" of eternity, the true first line in the Duque's
chronological history:

Se acabaron tus noches con su suelta cabellera de fogatas
y su gotear soñoliento y perenne de tamboriles,
en cuyo fondo te ibas hundiendo como en un lodo tibio
hasta llegar a las márgenes últimas de tu gran bisabuelo.

[Gone are your nights with their flowing hair of bonfire
and their drowsy, steady dripping of drums,
into whose depths you'd sink slowly as into warm mud
to the farthest shores of your great great-grandfather.]

As in several of Palés's poems, this one ends with a coda that
summarizes the entire trajectory, from the Duque's numinous origins to the present. As in "El Pozo," as well, the final stanza
comprises lines repeated from earlier stanzas.

From the farthest shores of your great great-grandfather,
across the hot flat silence of the plains,
why do your crocodiles weep in the far-off village on the Pongo,
Oh my fine, my honey-colored Duke of Marmelade!?

But here, one line undergoes a key semantic shift. The first image
of the plains refers to the giraffe's horizontal movement across
them. The same image appearing later turns the direction ninety
degrees so that the weeping of the crocodiles sails in a straight
line from the farthest point in the past, a "través del silencio
plano y caliente de las sabanas" ["across the hot flat silence of
the plains"], to the present. This geometric direction is an inverse
parallel to the Duke's passage, in a former tribal life, by way of
the drums, beyond the surface night to the "márgenes últimas"
of his ancestry. The "caimanes" cry because that original African
is lost. Unlike the soul of the dead "nené" in "Falsa Canción de
Baquiné," he will not return to Tembandumba. Unlike the dancing warrior in "Numen," the Duke will not dance his way to the
"negra formula esencial." Finally, unlike the poet himself who
descends into his own soul at the point that it fills with the frog-
like primal croaking, the essence of his poem, the Duque will not
travel to and encounter his own defining essence. The Duque is
lost in his inauthenticity.

Is this a racist poem? Is Palés's romantic interpretation of the
tribal African as a noble savage a bad thing—or simply an out-
dated one? Is being compared to an ape any different from being
compared to a frog, an ox, or a rooster? Is the Duke being ridiculed for underneath being like an ape, or was it for his aping
Westerners, or was it for his forsaking his numen? What makes

this poem so complicated is its presenting us all these questions intertwined. If we read it following the patterns of stylistic structures, however, we will begin to see that, whatever the adulterating, distasteful elements that still may detract from our reading, the poem's theme is the question of encountering authenticity. Underlying the poem is Palés's exterior/interior configuration and a passage to that interiority, a passage that throughout the body of his work Palés argues is inherently the moral thing to do. The Duke's sin of inauthenticity (of living on the exterior and forsaking his interiority) makes it impossible for him to return to his defining numen.

4

The Totemic Word

For Palés, the spiritual realm was a world beyond words. Between it and the mundane world, the world of sounds and silence, stands the doorway to the numinous world: the song without words, the poem. Thus, as the raw material of poetry, language is an ocean, one of whose shores laps that interiority called "alma," a medium to eternal numinous shores. Heideggerian in his thinking (a discussion on the probable, although unverified, influence of Heidegger, is reserved for the final chapter on the "Filí-Melé" poéms), Palés wrote poetry in order to listen to the language of Being: a conversation between his "alma" and the essence of things, ultimately encountered as words. For this reason, Palés portrays objects in the world as speaking a language that defines them, even if that language only consists of silence.

In the very early poem, "Soy Otro" ["I Am Another," 1918–1919], the speaker refers to the landscape as a mute language: "Yo conozco el lenguaje de labios del paisaje" ["I can read the lips of the landscape."] Likewise, the early "Esta Infancia" ["This Infancy"] portrays the decline of day as a sigh in which the speaker hears the sound of a goat or similar animal: "Suena un meee saludable en el desmayo diurno" ["A healthy braying sounds in the day's sigh."] Of that same period, "Los Ocios Pluviales" ("The Rainy Pastimes") employs a mouth image to describe the thirsty earth drinking as the rain falls making a monorhythmic sound:

> ¡Qué gusto tan sincero
> este de la absorción del agua fría
> por la tierra que está, poros abiertos,
> labios en calentura! Llueve. Llueve.
> Uaaa . . . interminablemente,
> sigue la monorritmia del uaueo.

[What a sincere delight
this absorption of cold water
by earth with pores open,
lips in heat! Rain. Rain.
Oooooaaoo . . . interminably,
the monorhythmic ooooaaooing.]

Similarly in "La Lluvia" the rain is described as a kind of song or sound into which the soul translates its story:

También en tu implacable canto que todo agobia
traduce el alma el cuento de los mejores días: . . .

[Also in your implacable song that exhausts everything
the soul translates the story of the best days.][1]

And lastly, in "Una Mañana de Rabi Jeschona" ("A Morning of Rabbi Jeschona") the dawn is described as speaking a language of its own:

La sombra compleja de signos y voces
aullaba su ronca ceguera de alba.

[The complex shadow of signs and voices
howls its hoarse dawn blindness.]

But language in Palés vision is also synonymous with a music. Thus, in "Los Animales Interiores," the speaker contemplates being able to understand and communicate the music of "a simple beast or any insect":

Y has de pensar entonces lo profundo que fuera
ser una bestia simple o un insecto cualquiera,
para absorber los jugos vitales y fecundos
y fluir en la cósmica vaharada de los mundos,
o tocado en tu vaga conciencia musical
hacer música bajo la imantación astral.

[And then you will wonder how profound to be
a simple beast or any insect,
so you can absorb the vital, fecund juices
and flow on the cosmic vapors of worlds,
or, touched in your hazy musical consciousness,
make music under the stars' magnetic pull.]

Also musical are the stylized languages of the pig and frog in "Danza Negra," whose sounds parallel the chanting of the Cocoroco and Cocoroca. In "Intermedios del Hombre Blanco," the frog's "cro-cro-cro," telescoping into a metaphor of an imponderable language, becomes the complex metaphor of the drumbeats whose message the white man cannot comprehend:

> Los oye el hombre blanco
> perdido allá en las selvas . . .
> Es un tuntún asiduo que se vierte
> imponderable por la noche inmensa.
>
> [Their sound reaches the white man
> bewildered far-off in the jungles . . .
> It's a ceaseless, divulging tomtom
> imponderable in the vast night.]

As seen in "Elegía del Duque de la Mermelada," Palés also metaphorically compares humans to animals in order to evoke a more basic form of nonverbal expression. In "¡Ay, Se Fue la Aldeana!" ("Ay, The Village Girl is Gone"), the country girl speaks her innocence through her eyes:

> en cuyos ojos, como en pado extenso
> bovinamente pasta la inocencia.
>
> [in whose eyes, as if in a wide meadow,
> innocence bovinely grazes.]

This association of human bodily expression with animal forms of communication operates in a subdued fashion in "Fantasías de la Tarde," in which the sailor's eyes, lips and bodies are portrayed as expressive creatures: "¿Qué dirán esos ojos tan enormes. . ." ["What must those so enormous eyes be saying. . ."]. The sailors' silent response to these questions is likened to the "mansedumbre" of oxen:

> Los marineros bajan las pupilas.
> Tienen esa obligada mansedumbre,
> de los bueyes que van a los pantanos
> a beber agua y a mirarse fúnebres.
>
> [The sailors lower their eyes.
> They possess that bound meekness
> of oxen who go to water holes
> to drink and exchange mournful stares.]

Human language as image and theme begins to appear in Palés's mature poems dating from 1920 on. In "Las Torres Blancas," for instance, the "Diosa-Poesía" speaks a language of "prophetic words" and creates a poetic rhythm with her gait. More subtly, in "Lullaby" the speaker "submerged in dream" through the language of poetry escapes the jaws of the "monstruos del hastío" ["the monsters of boredom"] who dwell in the "tierras malditas del silencio" ["damned lands of silence"].

In the book, *Canciones de la Vida Media* (1925), a frequent image of interiority is the primal "grito," sometimes depicted as a voice, which represents the language motive in that book. In this vein, in "El Dolor Desconocido" ("The Unknown Pain"), one of the several things the speaker calls the "dolor" is a "grito":

> gritos de auxilio, voces de socorro, gemidos,
> cual de un navío enorme que naufraga a lo lejos.

> [cries for help, voices of help, moans,
> as if an enormous ship was wrecked far away.]

The same distant voice cries out in the poem "El Sueño," in which the poet also makes an effort to use language by waving his arms:

> ¡Oh tú, que de tu propia realidad alejado
> fraguas, laboras, gritas, ridículo muñeco
> cuyos brazos inútiles se agitan en la sombra!

> [Oh you, who distanced from your own reality
> forges, works, screams, ridiculous doll
> whose arms uselessly flay in the shadows!]

Also in "Boca arriba":

> De pronto, un grito que arranca
> ¿de dónde? Y en él me anego.
> ¿De dónde (La luna es blanca
> como el ojo de un buho ciego).

> [Suddenly, a scream takes flight,
> from where? And I am drowning in it.
> From where? (The moon is white
> like a blind owl's eye.)]

And in "Topografía":

> y un grito allá en el fondo,
> como un hongo terrible y obstinado, . . .
>
> [and a scream, deepest down,
> like a fierce, unstoppable mushroom . . .]

In three of the poems in *Canciones*, however, we witness a major stylistic change. In "Los Animales Interiores," the only sound-image is musical, a "mustio violín." Also, in "Walhalla," a poem with a Wagnerian opera motif, the speaker walks through the Nordic dreamland listening to his own operatic singing voice.

> Tu canción solitaria de acentos guturales
> recorre las llanuras. Suenan cuernos marciales;
> rebrillan en la nubes los escudos guerreros; . . .
>
> [Your lone, guttural song
> echoes across the plains. Battle horns sound;
> warriors' shields glisten among the clouds. . .]

Imagined armies respond to his song that, as in "Pueblo Negro," is described by the phonological features of its lyrics, and "gritos" are heard, although these are not, as before, screams of despair but battle cries:

> gritos, hurras, blasfemias, rudo chocar de aceros . . .
> ¡El Walhalla! ¡El Walhalla! Los sombríos titanes
> hijos de las montañas, nietos de los volcanes,
> los colosos del bóreas que en batalla sangrienta,
> luchan con sorda brama dentro de la tormenta.
>
> [shouts, hurrahs, curses, angry clash of steel. . . .
> The Walhalla! The Walhalla! The shadowy titans
> sons of mountains, grandsons of volcanos,
> north wind giants who in bloody combat,
> clash with deafening groans in the storm.]

Eventually his song is reduced to the word "El Walhalla," which evokes and thus invokes the mythic numina and thus also transforms the tropics around the speaker:

> ¡El Walhalla! ¡El Walhalla! Tu canción resucita
> el recio mito nórdico por la landa infinita,

mientras a tus espaldas, como torvos chacales,
aúllan los terribles vientos septentrionales.

[The Walhalla! The Walhalla! Your song resurrects
the stout Nordic myth across the infinite land,
while at your back, like angry jackals,
howl the merciless Northern winds.]

Lastly, in "Sinfonía Nórdica" (discussed at greater length in other
contexts) the speaker's soul becomes filled with the images evoked
by Nordic composers, whose music invokes the numinous
"Walkirias."

The emergence of song and music and the sound images in
these three poems represents in *Canciones de la Vida Media* an
important transition in Palés's perception of language as spiritual
medium. The "grito" of the earlier, less mature poems, an image
of existential despair, is now replaced with a "canto" as the human sound that echoes in his soul. Similarly, too, language becomes synonymous with music. These changes, imaging the
chronology of Palés's poetic maturity, overlap with his handling
of the language imagery in *Tuntún de Pasa y Grifería*.

As discussed briefly in chapter 1, the linguistic consciousness
of *Tuntún* is expressed in the very title and underscored as the
book's key theme in the opening poem "Preludio en Boricua,"
which announces that the exotic-sounding language within is actually "Boricua." Mentioned at that time, the islands are described as "papamiento islands of volcano born" and "lands of
patois and papamiento." Also, Puerto Rico's "White linen aristocracy" in "Canción Festiva para Ser Llorada" is characterized by
its "bland and dripping language." But other important nuances
and techniques derived from Palés linguistic consciousness merit
further discussion and enrich our appreciation of that book.

In "Ñáñigo al Cielo," the jokes told in the Caribbean-bedecked
heaven are told in an extraterrestial lexicon:

> El buen humor celestial
> hace alegre despilfarro
> de chistes de muselina,
> en palabras que ha lavado
> de todo tizne terreno
> el cielo azul de los santos.
>
> [The celestial good humor
> cheerfully spreads around

bed sheet jokes,
in words washed clean
of all mundane filth
by the saints' blue heaven.]

God's language, on the other hand, is beyond the poet's ability to recreate in poetry:

(Palabra de Dios, no es música
transportable a ritmo humano,
lo que Jehová preguntara,
lo que respondiera el ñáñigo,
pide un más noble instrumento
y exige un atril más alto.

[God's word, isn't a music
playable to a human rhythm;
what Jehova may have asked,
what the *ñáñigo* answered,
begs a nobler instrument
and a higher music stand.]

In "Lagarto Verde," the Condesito is characterized by his willingness to say "yes": "a todos dice sí."[2] The woman in "Pueblo Negro" literally dissolves into the language of the lyrics of her song. In "Canción Festiva para Ser Llorada," Puerto Rican ruling society is described as speaking in "succulent metaphors" and "custard phrases." Also as part of this linguistic motive, as noted earlier, "canto" replaced the earlier "grito" and language became synonymous with music. In fact, throughout the book a broader circle of synonymous language imagery helps to reiterate the discourse of *Tuntún*. The song, for example, is an image of both the soul from which it emanates and the language of its lyrics. Language, synonymous with music, by extension becomes synonymous with dance. Hence, in *Tuntún* spirit, music, song, and language become semantically interchangeable. Thus, in "Ñáñigo al Cielo" Palés offers an image of God's language as a "música" that could not be played in "ritmo humano," while in "Preludio en Boricua" the soul is described as a music:

Y hacia un rincón—solar, bahía,
malecón o siembra de cañas—
bebe el negro su pena fría
alelado en la melodía
que le sale de las entrañas.

[And off in a corner—yard, bay,
seaside or cane field—
the black man drinks his sorrow cold,
stoned on the melody
seeping from his core.]

The synonymity of spirit-music-song-dance metaphors, on the one hand, and language on the other, also functions on a semantic level: language *evokes* its past and the dance ritual *invokes* the numen. Choosing a point at which evoke and invoke semantically intersect, Palés generates a totemic word device. A form of metonymy, by means of this totemic word device Palés evokes in the reader a consciousness of a word as both surface image and as vessel of essential numina, which can also be seen as the essence of linguistic and cultural legacy. The totemic word, then, invokes by evoking, and is both a medium of communication and a spiritual/historical legacy. Moreover, the totemic word device is also a stylistic expression of Palés's vision of the part as containing the whole. In "Canción de Mar," for instance, he claims that in order to possess the sea all he requires is a sponge: "Dadme esa esponja y tendré el mar" ["Give me that sponge and I'll have the sea"]. But as that poem also illustrates, that this study refers to Palés's word device as *totemic* should not mislead the reader into thinking that he employed it strictly in the Afro-Antillean poems. Rather the explicitness of the device in *Tuntún* helps us to appreciate once again Palés's consistency. "Walhalla," even though the fact wasn't identified when the poem was discussed earlier, is a poem entirely evoked from a totemic word, just as "la bomba" evoked "Timbuctú" and the imagined setting that comprises the poem.

The most prominent totemic words are historical allusions. In "Aires Bucaneros" ("Bucaneer Winds"), for example, whose very title evokes the spiritual activity in the cultural crosswinds of the Caribbean, historical allusions invoke the past that permeates the present:

D'Ogeron rige, Le Grand acecha,
Levasseur lucha con Pedro Sangre
y Morgan trama su obra maestra.

[D'Ogeron rules, Le Grand lurks,
Levasseur clashes with Pedro Blood
and Morgan schemes his masterpiece.]

Examples of historical allusions abound throughout Palés's work, notably in *Tuntún*.

A less evident use of the totemic word device is found in the poems inspired by Caribbean dances, a group discussed earlier on. In "Danza Negra," the totemic dance-word is the "mariyandá," whose "ritmo gordo" evokes the metaphorical dance of images. In "Bombo," the totemic dance-word is "la bomba," which opens the poem with an evocation of Timbucktu, which in turn evokes in the poet a tribe dancing around a campfire, invoking the numen "Bombo." The speaker is instantly transported to the event by the evocative powers of the dance-word "bomba," which descends to the poet from his linguisitic and cultural history. Originally referring to the instrument, the "bomba" or drum, the word today represents a specific style of dance and song, the remnant of the "bailes de bomba."[3] This link by way of a common linguistic history makes "hermanos" of the dancers in Timbucktu in the poem's mythic past, as well as of all who dance "bomba" or simply possess the word, for they have been inspirited by the same great numen, "Bombo," the title of the poem. Thus, the dance-word "bomba" evokes in the poet a scene of where the dance originally received its spiritual powers, a mythic etymology. Caribbean readers are also exhorted to join their spiritual kin and fortify their warrior spirit against the white man:

> Venid, hermanos, al balele.
> Bailad la danza del dios negro
> alrededor de la fogata
> donde arde el blanco prisionero.
> Que la doncella más hermosa
> rasgue su carne y abra el sexo,
> para que pase, fecundándola
> el más viril de los guerreros.
>
> Venid, hermanos, al balele.
> La selva entera está rugiendo.
> Esta es la noche de mandinga
> donde se forma un mundo nuevo.
> Duerme el caimán, duerme la luna,
> todo enemigo está durmiendo . . .
> Somos los reyes de la tierra
> que a Bombo, el Dios, sólo tenemos.
>
> [Come, brothers, to the feast.
> Dance to the black god,
> circling the tall flames
> where the white prisoner roasts.

Let the most beautiful maiden
scar her flesh and open her sex,
so the most virile warrior
may pass his plow, seeding her.

Come, brothers, to the feast.
All the jungle is roaring.
On this mandingo night
a new world dawns.
Asleep the cayman, asleep the moon,
asleep is our every enemy . . .
Kings of the earth are we
whose only God is Bombo.]

In "Majestad Negra," the dancing of the "rumba, macumba, candombe, bámbula" invokes the goddess Tembandumba, whose walk—a parallel of the Diosa-Poesía's rhythmic gait—is literally an incarnation of those dances:

Por la encendida calle antillana
—Rumba, macumba, candombe, bámbula—
va Tembandumba de la Quimbamba.

[Down the flaming Antillean street
—*Rumba, macumba, candombe, bámbula*—
walks Tembandumba from Farplace.]

"Candombe" is also the title of another poem. Manuel Alvarez Nasario informs us that the word *candombe* was originally employed "as a cry, let out at the start of the beating of the drums, indicating by it the start of bomba dance" (Alvarez Nasario, 310). Alvarez also points out that the "candombe" was once a war dance from which other dances eventually derived. Appropriately, the titular image "Candombe" introduces a poem in which a warrior dances against the evil magic of "la luna, el pez de plata, / la vieja tortuga maligna." As with "bomba" and "maríyandá," therefore, the "candombe" as both word and dance stands as the link between the present and its past, the mundane and the numinous.

In the four poems of the dance cycle, then, the device that Palés employs to establish the relation between the name of the dance and its evoked images is simple juxtaposition. As with the embedded "—*Rumba, macumba, candombe, bámbula*—," from the juxtaposition we must extrapolate the connection between the tribal dance and drumbeat and the names of the dances. Fortunately, as is often the case with Palés, to explain what is subdued in some poems we can find explicit examples in others. "Numen," for example, focuses on the "candombe" as an invocation of both the African and Antillean numina:

> Jungla africana—Tembandumba.
> Manigua haitiana—Macandal.
>
> [African jungle—Tembandumba.
> Haitian bush—Macandal.]

Macandal was, of course, the runaway slave who avenged other slaves and who, according to Haitian folklore, escaped death by becoming immortal, assuming many life forms. As inspiration for Haitian independence he was thus a numen. By juxtaposing him with Tembandumba and invoking both simultaneously, the "candombe" in the poem is two simultaneous *candombes*, one danced in Haiti and the other in Africa. But they are in fact the same dance, concurrent and sequential: the black man dancing in the "soledad," Palés's recurring pun on solitude and the tropics, invokes the "fórmula esencial," which at all historical periods and in any place is the same numinous source of "Nigricia" ("Blackland"). Likewise, of course, an Afro-Antillean poem that evokes through the *candombe* adds another ceremonial layer of participation, the poem itself invoking Macandal, Tembandumba and ultimately the same numinous essence of Nigricia.

In summary, the language of the mundane is also Palés's contact with the spiritual and, by means of unique instances of certain words, words that he interpreted as etymologically or psychologically totemic, he was transported to a spiritual state that also evoked the poem. This pattern is consistent throughout all the phases of his poetry. What changed with *Tuntún* was the cultural model. Palés began with a Western spiritual model of the passage of the soul to salvation, a separation between body and soul. This he then personalized into a poetic spirituality that allowed him contact with the soul directly through the poem. In *Tuntún*, therefore, he openly celebrated a form of spiritualism and thus depicted the contact with the atemporal destination as an ongoing interaction with the spiritual, the immediate intervention of the power of the "numen," a term that he first uses in *Tuntún*. But, as we shall see in the following chapter, stylistic patterns show that the notion of "numen" did not represent a conversion; rather, Palés started using the image because it described his own animistic, non-Western spiritual vision, another inheritance he doubtless ascribed to his African roots. The "numen," in semantic essence if not in surface word, is the hallmark of all of his poems.

5

Images of the Numen

In the pre-Afro-Antillean poems, we recall, the speaker submerges, leaps or flies to the superior reality beyond the surface mundane reality to an atemporal destination that as yet Palés did not call "numen." That atemporal destination was invariably depicted in several recurring images, some of which foregrounded the destination itself (the moon, the distant star) and others of which foregrounded the medium (the distant land, the dream) through which one passed. In *Tuntún de Pasa y Grifería*, however, the destination/passage images gave way to the "numen," which fused the medium and the destination, epitomizing Palés's vision of the physical realm as always in contact with the spiritual one. The "numen" in *Tuntún*, then, is an explicit rendering of the subdued numinous function of the destination images of the pre-Afro-Antillean poetry. Otherwise, the Palesian poetry structure remains unchanged: a passage, whether instant or slow, through the medium of the poem, to an encounter with the numinous. Both stages of numinous images are semantically synonymous. This parallel accounts for Palés's carrying the numen concept over to the post-*Tuntún* metaphysical poems and argues once again that the ostensible diversity in the stages of Palés's poetry is merely a surface variety that enriches his style as he consistently reiterates his discourse.

Luna/Estrella Lejana

Although not always explicitly an imagistic destination of a flight or passage, the moon is variously foregrounded as an enchanting object. "Las Torres Blancas" to which the speaker flies are bathed in a moonlight medium that causes "monstruos sublunares" to rise in the night air. In "Candombe" the warriors must elect someone to travel to the moon that telescopes into a metaphor of a silver tortoise releasing an evil spell as it swims in the black waters of the night (both water and night also being numinous images):

> La luna es tortuga de plata
> nadando en la noche tranquila.
> ¿Cuál será el pescador osado
> que a su red la traiga prendida:
> Sokola, Babiro, Bombassa,
> Yombofré, Bulón or Babissa?
> Tum-cutum, tum-cutum,
> ante la fogata encendida.
>
> Mirad la luna, el pez de plata,
> la vieja tortuga maligna
> echando al agua de la noche
> su jugo que duerme y hechiza . . .
> Coged la luna, coged la luna,
> traedla a un anzuelo prendida.
> Bailan los negros en la noche
> ante la fogata encendida.
> Tum-cutum, tum cu-tum,
> ante la fogata encendida.

> [A silver tortoise is the moon
> swimming in the placid night.
> Who'll be the daring fisherman
> to bring it caught in his net:
> Sokola, Babiro, Bombassa,
> Yombofré, Bulón or Babissa?
> *Tum-cutum, tum-cutum,*
> round the blazing bonfire.
>
> Look at the moon, the silver fish,
> the old, malignant tortoise
> oozing in night's water
> its lulling, bewitching broth . . .
> Catch the moon, catch the moon,
> bring it dangling from a hook.
> Black men dance in the night
> round the blazing bonfire,
> *Tum-cutum, tum cu-tum,*
> round the blazing bonfire.]

In "Claro de Luna," the speaker's heart, a frog, leaps into the night "de luna clara y tersa." Here the moonlight provides the conditions for the heart's passage to (and among) the stars:

¡Ah, que no llegue nunca la mañana!
¡Que se alargue esta lenta
hora de beatitud en que las cosas
adquieren una irrealidad suprema;

y en que mi corazón, como una rana,
se sale de sus ciénagas,
y se va bajo el claro de la luna
en vuelo sideral por las estrellas!

[Ah, let morning never come!
Never end the languor
of this blessed hour when things
assume a supreme unreality;

and when my heart, like a frog,
emerges from its swamp,
and takes off in the moonlight
on a star's flight among the stars!]

By foregrounding the moon's enchanting powers, these poems
give the impression that the moon inspires or causes flights to
distant points that are presumably distinct from the moon itself.
In the early poem "Lunomanía," for instance, a prefiguration of
"Claro de Luna," we see how the purity of the moon prompts
the speaker to desire to travel heavenward so he may become a
celestial body. The speaker relies on a synonymy between the
moon's purity and the "vivas / claridades" found in the heights
of the "escala luminosa":

Luna que haces soñar en bailarinas
vaporosas, aéreas, diamantinas . . . ,
dame la leche de tu jarra llena:
quiero ser de la altura, alba y serena.

Ser de los azahares que cultivas.
Quizá volverme estrella que dé vivas
claridades. ¿Entiendes? Deseo irme . . .
por tu escala lumínica subirme.

Le tengo mucho miedo a esta bajura.
¡Es tan impura. Y tú, ¡eres tan pura!
que quisiera escurrirme por tu vientre . . .

[Moon that makes me dream of dancers,
vaporous, aerial, diamond-bright . . . ,
give me the milk of your full pitcher:
I want to be of sky, dawn and serene.

Be of the orange blossoms you grow.
Maybe turn into a star to impart
bright clarity. Understand me? I want to depart . . .
up your luminous ladder.

I'm so afraid of this lowliness.
It is so impure! And you, you are so pure,
how I would slide into your womb . . .]

To take the argument one step further, the lunar influence to which the speaker in "Claro de Luna" attributes his heart's desire to fly among the stars (in other words, write a poem) in "El Destierro Voluntario" is credited exclusively to the star:

> Quiero purgar ¡oh montaña pagana!
> sobre tu roca mi lírico estigma,
> bajo la estrella escultora y lejana
> que le da al verso su forma y su enigma.

> [Upon your rock, oh pagan mountain,
> I want to wash off my lyrical stigma,
> under the distant, sculptor star
> that gives the poem its form and enigma.]

The star's inspiring poetry here makes explicit the semantic synonymy between the effects on the poet of any celestial body and that of the moon, a synonymy between celestial bodies that in "Lunomanía" is expressed implicitly and in "Claro de Luna" is completely absent from the surface text.

This synonymy also operates in two poems that, on the surface, employ completely unrelated images. In "El Pozo," the moon's influence causes the toad in the water's depths to croak, an act that fills the soul with "a remote sense of eternity." This feeling of being submerged in eternal waters is but a surface variation on the metaphorical flight through the heavens. "Canción de la Vida Media," as discussed in a previous chapter, employs an image of flight, with the star image as the destination, but before that flight the soul starts out compared to a tree, which must be pruned of the leaves of excess rhetorical devices. After the pruning, the tree is erect, clean and light, allowing the poet to telescope the tree into a pointed prow poised to set sail towards the heavens to the "estrella lejana":

> Así estás, alma mía, en tu grave hora nueva,
> toda desnuda y blanca,

> erguida hacia el silencio milenario y profundo
> de la estrella lejana.

> [So you stand, my soul, at your solemn new hour,
> completely bare and blank,
> erect toward the millenary, fathomless silence
> of the faraway star.]

Despite the surface impression that in "El Pozo" and "Canción de la Vida Media" the speaker is being transported to different destinations and in diametrically opposite directions, in both poems that destination is described as deep ("profundo") and timeless ("eterno") or virtually endless ('milenario"). Furthermore, in neither poem is the destination a fixed point: in "El Pozo" the destination is the water's depth, which suddenly becomes metaphorically open-ended, and in "Canción" the speaker's soul is bound for the "silencio milenario y profundo"— in other words, the space surrounding the distant star and not the star itself. Both images therefore are merely variations of the same limitless medium evoked by all the numinous images.

Sueño

Synonymous with the soul or dream world, the "sueño" image is Palés's most explicit medium image. Through the "sueño" the poet is transported to the eternal. The importance of the "sueño" as both image and experience is explained by the poem "El Sueño," discussed in a previous chapter, which avows that "El sueño es el estado natural" ["The dream is the natural state"]. But "sueño" is amorphous stuff, an abstraction, which generates more abstraction. Thus we frequently encounter the "sueño" image embodied in another, more concrete image, such as water in "El Sueño" above:

> ese ras de agua inmóvil perennemente mudo,
> muy allá de los límites del espacio y el tempo.

> [that stagnant water surface, perennially mute,
> far beyond the shores of space and time.]

"Lullaby" resorts to a subdued allusion to water, as the speaker travels submerged in dream. On the other hand, in "Lunomanía" the "bailarinas" evoked by the moon are really *sueños*.

One underlying numen feature of the "sueño" image, whether explicit or subdued, is that it evokes both a sense of place and of being transported to another place. This dual sense operates in both "Pueblo Negro" and "Las Torres Blancas," in which the "sueño" is simultaneously medium and the encountered dream object. The "Pueblo Negro" is described as being "de sueño" and "caserío irreal de paz y sueño," where "irreal" refers to a superior unmundane reality. "Las Torres Blancas," the black town's parallel, is a dream city in a nocturnal countryside indistinguishable from the dream itself.

This capacity of "sueño" to evoke simultaneously a changed state or the medium to that state is also demonstrated in "Canción de Mar,"[1] a poem that employs a numinous water image to provide a depth that telescopes into a dreamscape cluttered with dream images that are encountered in other changed media in Pales's poems. The sea depths, referred to as the "imperio fabuloso," becomes a metaphor of "sueño":

> Abajo es el imperio fabuloso:
> la sombra de galeones sumergidos
> desangrando monedas de oro pálido y viejo;
> las conchas entreabiertas como párpados
> mostrando el ojo ciego y lunar de las perlas;
> el pálido fantasma de ciudades hundidas
> en el verdor crepuscular del agua . . .
> remotas ulalumes de un sueño inenarrable
> resbalado de monstuos que fluyen en silencio
> por junglas submarinas y floras de trasmundo.
>
> [Below is the fabulous empire:
> shadows of submerged galleons
> bleeding old, faded doubloons;
> conches half-open like eyelids
> revealing blind, moon-bright pearl eyes;
> the pale ghosts of sunken cities
> in the water's twilight green . . .
> remote Ulalumes of an indescribable dream
> slimy with monsters soundlessly weaving
> through submarine jungles and afterlife flora.]

Agua, Mar, Noche

As "Canción de Mar" also demonstrates, the passage to the nether or distant world is frequently depicted as a movement through water or a watery substance. We have also seen the speaker in "Lullaby" refer to his being "submerged" in the dream and, in "El Sueño," to mundane existence as a light splash on the water's surface. In "Pueblo," a water image is at first suggested, with the mayor "dabbling" in his life, and later expressed explicitly, as the poet urges some scoundrel to come to the town and throw a stone against "el agua muerta de sus vidas."

One of the most complex constructions in Pales's imagistic repertory is the series of images telescoped from the simple image of water as the medium to the soul-world. The prototype of this series is found in "El Pozo," a poem that compares the soul to the "pozo" ("well") in whose depths a toad croaks. Taking the "pozo" as one element (the toad being the other), we notice that in some poems the "pozo de agua" is compared to the night, as occurs in "Voces del Mar": "bajo la noche hueca como un pozo infinito" ["under the hollow night like an infinite well"]. And that same "pozo infinito" drips down on mundane reality from overhead in "Nocturno" ("Nocturn"), in which the insomniac poet contemplates the stillness of the night with its "luna acuosa" ("watery moon"):

> El silencio es tan hondo y las cosas están
> tan sensibles, tan vagas, tan aéreas, tan frágiles,
> que si yo diera un grito caerían las estrellas
> húmedas sobre el parque.
>
> Hay que estar quieto, quieto, pues cualquier ademán
> tendría una alargada repercusión unánime . . .
> —Como una gota densa y profunda, en la noche,
> la hora, remota, cae.

> [So abysmal is the silence and things feel
> so tender, so vague, so aerial, so fragile,
> that if I were to let out a scream, stars would rain
> wet over the park.
>
> One has to keep still, still, lest any movement
> cause a protracted reaction all at once . . .
> —Like a dense, huge drop, in the night,
> somewhere distant the hour falls.]

Similarly, the toad submerged in the "pozo" appears in several poems. In "Topografía" a toad is submerged in the metaphorical "pozo infinito" of the night:

La noche cierra pronto y en el lúgubre
silencio rompe el sapo
su grito de agua oculta que las sombras
absorben como tragos.

[Night shuts down early and in the gloomy
silence, toads blurt out their croak,
gurgling an underground water
the shadows gulp like drinks.]

In this region, the toad's "grito de agua oculta," which only emerges at night, is one of the few sources of water, which semantically signifies spiritual vitality. During the day, the only water around is shallow and stagnant:

El sol calienta en las marismas rojas
el agua como un caldo,
y arranca del arenal caliginoso
un brillo seco y áspero.

[The sun in the red marshes heats
the water like a broth,
and from dark sandy patches extracts
a cragged, dry shine.]

The toad in the well is also the prototype of the reptilian drums in the night of "Intermedios del Hombre Blanco" ("White Man's Interludes"):

La noche es un criadero de tambores
que croan en la selva,
con sus roncas gargantas de pellejo
cuando alguna fogata los despierta.

[Night is a breeding ground of drums
whose hoarse throats of skin
croak throughout the jungle
when awakened by a bonfire.]

Knowing that the night, like a huge well, also has the attributes of a huge soul adds to our evoked sense of spiritual weight on the shoulders of the white man lost in the jungle (from which, nightly, the Afro-Antillean numina, demons to the white man, emerge). Like the toad's croaking in the water or the black woman's sensual body-song dissolving in the atmosphere of

"Pueblo Negro," the sound of the "tambores" pervades the night air:

> Con soñoliento gesto de batracios
> alzan pesadamente la cabeza,
> dando al cálido viento la pringosa
> gracia de su eneregía tuntuneca.

> [With drowsy amphibian faces
> heavily they lift their heads,
> lending the warm breeze the oily
> grace of their drumming energy.]

Steeped in the night, the white man is chased by the "tambores" that, although reptilian, have stingers that can get into his interior self and contaminate his soul with their contagious musical "cró-cró":

> ¡Ahí vienen los tambores!
> Ten cuidado, hombre blanco, que a ti llegan
> para clavarte su aguijón de música.
> Tápate las orejas,
> cierra toda abertura de tu alma
> y el instinto dispón a la defensa;
> que si en la torva noche de Nigricia
> te picara un tambor de danza o guerra,
> su terrible ponzoña
> correrá para siempre por tus venas.

> [Here come the drums!
> White man, watch out they don't reach you
> to nail you with their music-making stinger.
> Cover your ears,
> close every opening in your soul
> and ready your reflexes in defense;
> for in the fierce Blackland night
> should a war or dance drum prick you,
> its savage venom
> will flow in your veins forever.]

The three-element telescoped metaphor made up of alma-pozo-noche—along with other numinous images—operates in "A Luis Lloréns Torres" to create both the medium in which a *coquí*, the tiny Puerto Rican tree frog, whistles in the night and the medium through which the poet Lloréns submerges to reach the heavenly spheres and the "origen de las primeras cosas":

Y más allá, en el fundo, en la paz anchurosa
y vegetal del campo, cuando la soledosa
voz del coquí, goteando de la nocturna calma
bajaba hasta el hondón elemental de tu alma . . .

[And farther off, in your country space, in the wide,
vegetal rural peace, as the *coquí*'s
solitary voice, dripping from the night's calm,
fell to the elemental bottom of your soul . . .]

Another key recurring water image, as noted earlier, is the sea. In "El Dolor Desconocido" ("The Unknown Pain"), for example, like the water in "El Pozo," the sea is a metaphor of the soul:

A veces, de sus roncos altamares ocultos,
de esas inexploradas distancias, vienen ecos
tan vagos, que se pierden como ondas desmayadas
sobre una playa inmóvil de bruma y de silencio.

[A times, from their hoarse, unseen seas,
from those unexplored reaches, arrive echoes
so dim they dissolve like waves that flatten
against an immovable shore of mist and silence.]

As a metaphor for the soul, the sea is also portrayed as being influenced by the numinous moon, as the well-water was in "El Pozo." This effect of the moon on the water-soul-sea is seen in "Voces del Mar":

A medianoche escuchan gritos, y se levantan
medrosos. De la luna baja un silencio astral;
el mar se tiende vasto y azul; las aguas cantan;
cunde el retumbo de la armonía sideral . . .

[At midnight they hear shouts, and rise from bed
trembling. From the moon descends a star's silence;
the sea extends vast and blue; the waters sing;
everywhere a starry harmony resounds.]

Different from the "pozo," the sea image contributes its capacity to evoke a sense of horizontal infinity that provides the medium for the image of a long sea voyage. In a few cases, however subdued the metaphors, this sea voyage image is obvious. In "San Sabás," for instance, the subdued metaphor of the night as a sea obviously becomes the medium across which the "peñón colosal"

("colossal rock") will travel into the heavens "como una proa espi-
ritual" ("like a spiritual prow"). But a subdued long sea voyage
image is also central to "Elegía del Duque de la Mermelada," in
which the Duque in a former life is depicted as being transported
by his ritualistic dances on the banks of the Pongo river through
the wet night to the "farthest shores" where he encounters his
numinous "great-great grandfather."

This subdued voyage parallels the explicit one referred to in
"El Llamado," in which, no matter where the speaker turns, he
encounters the call to voyage across a sea. At first, he is looking
at a real sea:

> Estoy frente a la mar y en lontananza
> se va perdiendo el ala de una vela;
> va yéndose, esfumándose,
> y yo también me voy borrando con ella.
>
> [I'm facing the sea and in the horizon
> a wing-shaped sail fades from view;
> it continues to dissolve, turning to smoke,
> and I erase myself as it does.]

Later his lover's eyes also become a metaphorical sea calling the
called one inexorably "allá":

> Mas de pronto, despierta,
> y allá en el negro hondón de sus pupilas
> que son un despedirse y una ausencia,
> algo me invita a su remota margen
> y dulcemente, sin querer, me lleva.
>
> [But suddenly she awakes,
> and far in the black fathoms of her pupils,
> at once a departure and an absence,
> something invites me to her distant shore
> and, helpless, I am lovingly taken there.]

Finally, resigned—or sounding resigned—to his fate, he describes the sea he will sail:

> Un mar hueco, sin peces,
> agua vacía y negra
> sin vena de fulgor que la penetre
> ni pisada de brisa que la mueva.
> Fondo inmóvil de sombra,
> límite gris de piedra . . .

[A hollowed-out sea, fishless,
a vacant, black water
with no brilliant ray to enter it,
nor breeze's step to ripple it.
Motionless floor of shadow,
gray limit of stone.]

Lejano País (Distant Country)

On the surface, the "lejano país" is one of the destination images at the end of the speaker's long voyage. In "A Un Amigo," he arrives at the "lejano país" by way of the sea. In "Voz de lo Sedentario y lo Monótono," the speaker in a wheelchair imagines himself travelling to it in a landau. An earlier version of "Voz," titled "Tic-Tac," however, demonstrates that, on a semantic level, the "lejano país" is actually a metaphor for the envisioned dream-soul world and, by extension, for eternity. In that early poem,[2] the speaker not only has a vision of the "lejano país" but of the dream city found in it, the same city encountered in "Las Torres Blancas." Also, as in the later poem, in "Tic-Tac" the speaker spiritually flies there:

> Y otear en los confines la ciudad prometida;
> el lazareto blanco para las penas malas,
> y previvir la vida dormida de esa vida
> más puro el sentimiento y más firmes las alas.

> [And envisage in the horizon the promised city,
> the white quarantine for harsh sentences,
> and imagine the sleepy life in that life,
> purer my perceptions and firmer my wings.]

Only after waiting a long time for that vision, when the speaker is virtually convinced that the vision will be a failure does "Ella" (a prefiguration of the Diosa-Poesía) arrive from the dream city in the "lejano país."

But unlike the other pre-Afro-Antillean numinous images, the "lejano país" rarely appears in the surface text of the mature poems, in which this image appears subdued in other images. In "El Llamado," the "lejano país" is pointed to by the adverb "allá" ("far-off"). In "El Dolor Desconocido," it is the "ciudad dormida" ("sleeping city"). In "A Gloria Madrazo Vicens," it is the ultimate destination of the speaker's own "último viaje sin regreso" ["final trip without return"]. In "Puerto al Tiempo en Tres Voces" ("Entrance to Time in Three Voices") that place is alluded to as "ribera" ("shore").

Also, every instance of the "lejano país" image, whether explicit (in early poems) or subdued (in the mature poems), is part of an extended image that evokes a sense of passage. That "país" only exists as an unattainable destination or vision whose very impossibility makes the dream or poem necessary as a medium to it, and only the numen, the dead and the poet experience the journey. Hence in "A Luis Lloréns Torres," the "lejano país" is the "cósmico imperio" ("cosmic empire") to which the dead poet used to travel when pondering metaphysical questions and now will reach in death. In "Boceto," the antecedent of "tú" is really the Essence of Poetry, described as "vuelo hacia país flotante" [flight to a floating country"]. In "Majestad Negra," the goddess Tembandumba is from the "Quimbamba," an African-derived word meaning "país lejano" (see Alvarez Nasario, 231), which in popular speech signifies a remote unspecified place, into whose realm the Antillean street has semantically been transported by means of the *"rumba, macumba, candombe, bámbula."*

Numina, Deities, Atmosphere

The "numen," as indicated earlier, replaced the manifold spiritual and medium (to a spiritual encounter) images in the pre-Afro-Antillean poems. This shift to the numen concept changed the emphasis of Pales's vision: whereas in earlier works one experiences a sense of passage to the spiritual realm, a voyage that came about either under the spell of celestial bodies or from a desire that emerges from the nether-soul world, in *Tuntún* what is emphasized is the process of *return* to origins or an *immediate contact* with that numinous source.

To illustrate, in "Falsa Canción de Baquiné" ("False Child's Wake Song") the baby's death is depicted as a return across a superficially unimaged sea to the beach where the maternal Tembandumba awaits:

> Pero que ahora verá la playa.
> Pero que ahora verá el palmar.
> Pero que ahora ante el fuego grande
> con Tembandumba podrá bailar.

[But now he will see the beach.
But now he will see palm trees.
But now round the great fire
he can dance with Tembandumba.

Tembandumba and Bombo are the two most frequently invoked numina in *Tuntún*. Tembandumba also appears in "Nam-Nam," a poem that explodes by exaggeration the former Western racist convention that depicted "Dark Africa" as a chomping mouth devouring a meal of white missionaries and explorers:

> Quien penetró en Tangañica
> por vez primera—ñam-ñam;
> quien llegó hasta Tembandumba
> la gran matriarca—ñam-ñam.

> [Who was the first to penetrate
> to Tanganyica—*ñam-ñam*
> who reached Tembandumba,
> the great matriarch—*ñam-ñam.*]

Consumed by the natives, the white man's penetration therefore extended to the great goddess and matriarch Tembandumba.

In "Majestad Negra" ("Black Majesty"), Tembandumba personifies the totemic Antillean dances. Invoked by the "rumba, macumba, candombe, bámbula," Tembandumba descends on the hot Antillean streets. As an anthropomorphism, she is sensuality incarnate and her dance movements are rendered in a metaphor of a sugar mill grinding out sugar and molasses:

> Culipandeando la Reina avanza,
> y de su inmensa grupa resbalan
> meneos cachondos que el gongo cuaja
> en ríos de azúcar y de malaza.
> Prieto trapiche de sensual zafra,
> el caderamen, masa con masa,
> exprime ritmos, suda que sangra,
> y la molienda culmina en danza.

> [Curvaceous behind, the Queen advances
> as down her huge rump drip
> sexual jiggles the conga curds
> in rivers of cane juice and molasses.
> Blackened sugar mill for a sensual harvest,
> her great thighs, mass against mass,

>   squeeze out rhythms, sweat clear blood,
>   and the grinding culminates in dance.]

In this poem, Tembandumba from the "Quimbamba" ("Farplace")
exists as both a surface image of an earthy black woman and a
semantic image of the goddess.

In "Falsa Canción de Baquiné," the great god Bombo escorts
the dead baby's "zombí," or resurrected corpse, back to Guinea:

>   Y a la Guinea su zombí vuelva . . .
>   —Coquí, cocó, cucú, cacá—
>   Bombo el gran mongo bajo la selva
>   su tierno paso conducirá.

>   [And to Guinea his zombi returns . . .
>   —*Coquí, cocó, cucú, cacá*—
>   Bombo the great god of the jungle
>   will lead his baby steps.]

Bombo also lends his name to the title of the poem "Bombo,"
in which he is instantly invoked by the dance "la bomba," used
here by Palés as a totemic word (see chapter 5) that evokes both
the original drum and the dance it inspired. Ambiguously, both
meanings of "bomba" invoke the great numen "Bombo":

>   La bomba dice:—¡Tombuctú!
>   Cruzan las sombras ante el fuego.
>   Arde la pata del hipopótamo
>   en el balele de los negros.
>   Sobre la danza Bombo rueda
>   su ojo amarillo y soñoliento,
>   y el bembe de ídolo africano
>   le cae en cuajo sobre el pecho.
>   ¡Bombo del Congo, mongo máximo,
>   Bombo del Congo está contento.

>   [The *bomba* says:—Timbucktu!
>   Shadows crisscross before the fire.
>   Leg of hippo roasts
>   at the black tribe's feast.
>   Above the dancing, Bombo rolls
>   his yellow, dreaming eyes,
>   and his African-idol lip
>   thickly sags over his chest.
>   Bombo of the Congo, highest god,
>   Bombo of the Congo is now happy.]

Besides God, other Western deities are invoked in Palés's work. Three poems employ the image of the Valkyrie, the handmaiden of the Nordic god Odin, who carry off the slain warriors to their rightful place in the Valhalla, another "lejano país." In "Walhalla," the poet imagines himself in a Nordic setting superimposed over his own Antillean town. Speaking to himself, he acknowledges that his song resurrects the ancient Nordic myth, an acknowledgment that the poem, on the semantic level, opens a door to the myth's spiritual dimension. Similarly, the Valkirie is mentioned in "Sinfonía Nórdica," which consists of five stanzas each composed of Nordic images evoked by the music of five different European composers, a process that culminates in the chant of the Valkyrie, which transports the poet once again to the spiritual realm. Finally, it is to the Valkyrie that Palés compares his own Antillean myth, the *mulata-antilla:*

> En potro de huracán pasas cantando
> tu criolla canción, prieta walkiria,
> con centelleante espuela de relámpagos
> rumbo al verde Walhalla de las islas.

> [On a hurricane colt you ride by singing
> your creole song, dark Valkirie
> with lightning spurs flashing,
> bound for the green Valhalla of the islands.]

(Observe the ambiguity created by the omission of a comma after "relámpagos." Both the Valkirie and the "lightning" are "bound for . . . ," the latter's destination being the islands praised as heavenly and the former's being the heaven that watches over the islands. Thus the image operates on both a mundane and spiritual level simultaneously.)

Other numina-gods in *Tuntún* are given less auspicious treatments: the warrior numen papá Ogún is invoked in "Falsa Canción"; Ecué, Changó, papá Abasí and papá Bocó in "Lamento"; the unnamed "gran bisabuelo" of the Duque de la Mermelada in the "Elegía." Along with Tembandumba and Bombo, these numina compose the pantheon of ancestral African spirits that are invoked by the Caribbean music, dance and language. They are also the unspecified "demonios" that, invoked by the "tambores" in "Intermedios del Hombre Blanco," descend upon the white man:

> A su conjuro hierven
> las oscuras potencias:

> fetiches de la danza,
> tótemes de la guerra,
> y los mil y uno demonios que pululan
> por el cielo sensual del alma negra.
>
> [At their conjuring
> the dark powers swarm;
> fetishes for the dance,
> totems for war,
> and the thousand and one teeming demons
> across the black soul's sensual heaven.]

A major juxtaposition of theistic conventions occurs in "Ñáñigo al Cielo," in which a *ñáñigo*, a member of a secret society of black Cubans, rises to the heaven of the Western God. An excellent example of Palés's antipoetic aesthetic, mixing humor with seriousness, on the surface "Ñáñigo al Cielo" is like a graphically spectacular cartoon of heaven's celebrating the event by turning itself into a Caribbean paradise. Behind the wit and imagery, however, the poem inquires about the fate of black souls in a white heaven. Besides the surface anthropomorphic goings on, stylistically what takes place is that the Western God, implicit in Palés's non-Afro Antillean allusions to eternity and the soul, now joins his pantheon of myth and imagistic numina, a white tribal counterpart to the great Bombo:

> De pronto Jehová conmueve
> de una patada el espacio.
> Rueda el trueno y quedan solos
> frente a frente, Dios y el ñáñigo.
> —En la diestra del Señor,
> agrio foete, fulge el rayo.
>
> [Suddenly Jehova quakes
> the cosmos with one kick.
> Thunder rolls, and face to face,
> God and the ñáñigo are alone.
> —In the Lord's right hand,
> a sharp whip, lightning flashes.]

The speaker admits that God's utterances to the *ñáñigo* are in a language that "no es música / transportable a ritmo humano" ["isn't a music / playable to a human rhythm"]. All he can claim to know are the signs perceived by his senses. His sight does see them embrace and his sense of smell detects that their embrace emits an odor of Antillean rum that engulfs the pair and evokes a festive air:

> Pero donde el pico es corto,
> vista y olfato van largos,
> y mientras aquélla mira
> a Dios y al negro abrazados,
> éste percibe un mareante
> tufo de ron antillano,
> que envuelve las dos figuras
> protagonistas del cuadro,
> da tonos de cumbancha
> al festival del espacio).

> [But where the beak is short,
> sight and smell go farther,
> and while the former sees
> God and the black man hugging,
> the latter smells a dizzying
> whiff of Antillean rum,
> which engulfing the scene's
> two principle players,
> adds a tone of good times
> to the cosmic get-together.]

The result, of course, is a spiritual communion that mythically defines the Caribbean, the same *mulatez* celebrated in "Mulata-Antilla" and "Ten con Ten."

The product of that embrace is also a telescoped metaphor of perhaps the most subtle of the images of the numinous presence: *atmósfera*. A transformation of the water image, the dense humid atmosphere—etymologically a "sphere of vapor"— threads all the phases of Palés's work by evoking throughout his work a sense of a dream-soul state. In the non-Afro-Antillean poems we encounter both explicit and subdued examples in "Walhalla," "Humus," "Las Torres Blancas," and "Los Animales Interiores," to name a few. In *Tuntún,* the "atmósfera" becomes the collective Caribbean medium charged with African ancestral numina, an air that Palés perceived as spiritually haunted. As in the non-Afro-Antillean poems, the image is often used explicitly as itself and other times is transformed into images of sound, smell or heat, as is illustrated above in "Ñáñigo al Cielo." Other examples were previously discussed in "Pueblo Negro," "Canción Festiva para Ser Llorada," "Intermedios del Hombre Blanco," and "Mulata-Antilla."

As with all the other numen images, the "atmósfera" is quite literally another *sphere*, an "allá" inhabited by a spiritual source, the object of Palés's recurring poetic encounter. Satisfactorily naming or defining or possessing that object is, of course, impossible. The quest generates the poem, the altar on which we fleetingly understand the enigmatic and see the unseeable. Through the poem Palés can only recreate a sense of the encounter with this "irrealidad," a sense recreated not only through imagery. For the numen images also come to our consciousness as predicate nominatives of an impersonal and undefined "es," which give them the quality of a causeless existence, an emergence, an apparition. An important component of Palés's imagery was, as will be discussed in chapter 6, the grammatical pattern of his style.

6

A Grammar of Palés' Style

Syntax of Encounter

The dominant syntax that Palés Matos used in his poems is—whether explicit or subdued—the copulative verb (either *ser* or *estar*) followed by the predicate nominative. It is the syntax of naming things or recording the speaker's sense of immediacy, lending the poem a sense of encounter. In Palés's style, this syntax has several transformations. Frequently the syntax is patent in the surface structure: "La noche es un criadero de tambores" ["Night is a breeding ground of drums"]. At other times, the poem itself actually functions as an extended predicate nominative of an implicit sentence whose subject is the title.

"Danza Negra" is an effective model. This poem consists of a catalogue of images evoked by the totemic dance-word "mariyandá." The images themselves become dancers participating in a "Danza Negra"; all the images, however, are predicate nominatives of a subdued sentence whose subject is the title "Danza Negra." In other words, we can read the poem as a sentence stating that *Una danza negra es . . .* all the images represented by the catalogue of noun phrases that make up the body of the poem. Hence the "Calabó y bambú" are implicitly preceded by the copulative *ser* that is missing in the surface text. Similarly the "Gran Cocoroco" and his queen are also part of an extended predicate nominative. These more complex images really consist of restricted relative clauses:

> |Es| El Gran Cocoroco |que| dice: tu-cu-tú.
> |Es| La Gran Cocoroca |que| dice: to-co-tó.

The verb is dropped because in both instances the relation of the images to "Danza" is intentionally subdued: the images instantly dance, "are" the "danza." But this implicit "ser" rises to the surface in a few lines that open with "Es": "Es el sol de hierro que

115

arde en Tombuctú. / Es las danza negra de Fernando Póo." Observe how in the following parallel constructions the first couplet includes the *ser*, while in the second couplet the *ser* is subdued:

> Es la raza negra que ondulando va
> en el ritmo gordo del mariyandá.
>
> El alma africana que vibrando está
> en el ritmo gordo del mariyandá.

This syntactic pattern, of course, is also consistent with the one in his non-Afro-Antillean poems. "Sinfonía Nórdica" also consists of evoked images, this time elicited by the speaker's contemplation of the music of certain Northern European composers. Again, disregarding the subject function of the title (and its ironic punning: *sin fonía nórdica*, or without Nordic voice), the poem is structured as a catalog of images that are predicate nominatives; the syntactic structure is identical to that of "Danza Negra," with every stanza an extended noun phrase. Unlike that poem, however, "Sinfonía Nórdica" shows no surface evidence of *ser* being the verb linking the title-subject to the body of the poem. And what makes this poem especially difficult to analyze syntactically are the final lines of the first five stanzas, in which the composers are mentioned. Here the semantic relation of the composers to three preceding lines is left up to whatever semantic connections the reader can evoke by the juxtaposition. Take the second stanza as an example:

> Lagos donde solloza la náyade taimada
> para extraviar al lento burgrave solitario
> que entre la niebla, al paso de sus renos, avanza.
> —Offenbach: risa de agua, ritonelo de encanto—.
>
> [Lakes where the cunning naiad moans
> to mislead the slow, solitary burgher
> who in blowing snow, at his reindeer's pace, presses on.
> —Offenbach: smile of water, bewitching refrain—.]

The five key images in this poem ("Bosques escandinavos," "Lagos," "Ruiseñor," "Bahía groenlandesa," and "Danza del duende oblongo") compose a nordic pastoral setting that the music symphonically evokes. For this reason, a syntactic rewrite of this poem establishes a copulative relation between the title, the composite of core images and the composer:

|Una sinfonía nórdica| |es| |se va componiendo de|

Bosques escandinavos . . .

|Y| Lagos . . . |que evoca la música de|
Offenbach, risa de agua, ritornelo de encanto.

[|A Nordic symphony| |is| |consists of|

Scandinavian forests . . .

|And| Lakes . . . |that are evoked by]
—Offenbach, laughter of water, bewitching refrain—

In the final stanza, bringing to the surface the only evidence of a copulative relation between the stanzas, the copulative conjunction "Y" extends the catalog, adding another music: the voices of the Valkiries. The "Y," however, does not immediately introduce the stanza's dominant image, which is reserved for the third line:

Y de pronto, en la landa silenciosa y dormida
(grandes bosques oscuros, quietas llanuras blancas)
rompe el huracanado tropel de las Walkirias
con rumbo a los remotos confines del Walhalla.

[And, suddenly, over the silent, sleeping land
(great dark forests, soundless snow-blank plains)
blow the hurricane fury of the Valkiries
off to the distant reaches of the Valhalla.]

The core image is, of course, the chorus of the numinous "Walkirias." What evokes/invokes these numina is the catalogue of metaphors that the poem has been composing from the images evoked by the different composers. Ultimately, that the composers become the presence of the Valkiries completes the catalogue and the composite symphony.

A third model of this stylistic syntax is "Canción de Mar," which consists of a catalogue of stanzas in which each is a predicate nominative. Different from the previous poems, "Canción" employs a refrain device used to intensify the copulative sense throughout the poem. Hence the most prominent refrained element, the line "Dadme una esponja y tendré el mar" ["Give me a sponge and I'll have the sea"] coheres by force of the copulative conjunction that equates the figurative few drops of water with the possession of the entire sea. And about the sea, the stanzas (those that open the refrained line) go on to predicate that the sea is the sum of all the evoked images. These stanzas predicate in two ways. In some cases the line following the refrained line deletes the "mar" in its imbedded sentence and in other cases it does not. This is so because when the repeated "mar" precedes a noun (such as in "|El mar que es un| Jornalero del cosmos," the resulting surface transformation would be the redundant, poetically weaker "el mar, un jornalero," (from which the "un" would be deleted). The same is also true of "Peón de confianza" and "Hércules prodigioso."

In contrast, the opposite occurs in the lines where predicate adjectives are used. The surface transformation "el mar en overol azul" ["the sea in blue overalls"] and "el mar infatigable, el mar rebelde" ["the indefatigable, the rebel sea"] are left at that stage because deleting "el mar," however redundant on the semantic level, would result in the imagistically weaker, unclear and imageless lines composed entirely of modifier(s). The result would be the following distortion:

> Dadme esa esponja y tendré el mar.
> En overol azul
> abotonado de islas . . .

> Dadme esa esponja y tendré el mar.
> Infatigable, rebelde,
> contra su sino de forzado eterno, . . .

> [Give me that sponge and I'll have the sea.
> In blue overalls
> buttoned with islands . . .

> Give me that sponge and I'll have the sea.
> Inexhaustible, rebellious,
> against its destiny of eternal bondage. . . .]

Stanzas four and five open without the refrain and thus are not juxtaposed to the word "mar." Their function in the poem requires that the reader make certain associations. Extending the circus image in the third stanza, for example, the fourth employs the imperative case of "Ver" to focus our attention on the myriad activities in the "circo":

> (Ved el tifón oblicuo y amarillo de China,
> con su farolería de relámpagos
> colgándose a la vela de los juncos.
> Allá el monzón, a la indostana,
> el pluvioso cabello perfumado de sándalo
> y el yatagán del rayo entre los dientes,

arroja sus eléctricas bengalas
contra el lujoso paquebote
que riega por las playas de incienso y cinamomo
la peste anglosajona del turismo. . . .

[Observe the slanted, yellow typhoon from China,
with its lightning-flame lanterns
hanging from the sails of junks.
Over there, as in Hindustan, the monsoon,
its rain hair fragrant with sandalwood
and a scimitar bolt between clenched teeth,
hurls its electrical fireworks
at the opulent pack-boat
that along incense and cinnamon beaches
spreads the plague of Anglo-Saxon tourists . . .]

As is evident from the above stanza four, three lines deviate from the syntax before returning to it in line four: "Allá está el monzón. . . ." After that, stanza five deviates from the dominant syntax even longer. The point being made is that this third model, "Canción de Mar" represents the kind of poem that uses the syntax as a standard against which to introduce a contrasting syntax, a deviation of tone.

Lastly on the subject of syntax, it should be underscored that this treatment of Palés's syntactical pattern is a simplified model. A thorough description of even the three quoted poems would require a much longer treatment than would be practical in this analysis. The important point to underscore is the diverse ways in which Palés transforms a single syntactic pattern. By identifying this pattern the reader will better appreciate Palés's proclivity for naming, for encountering as if for the first time.

Adverbials

As the *copulative + predicate nominative* syntax heightens our sense of encounter, the prominent key adverbials outline the configuration of the evoked passage to the object of encounter. Perhaps the best evidence of the importance of adverbials is demonstrated by the small yet significant changes that differentiate "Elegía del Duque de la Mermelada" from its prefiguration "Elegía del Saltimbanqui" (both discussed in chapter 3). Both poems open with almost identical elegiac exclamations. And both proceed from there to contrast their respective character's past from his present state, down to the lexical detail of employing the impersonal use of "acabar" to draw a bold line between previous and present states:

> Se acabó tu alegría, terminó tu cabriola.
>> "Elegía del Saltimbanqui"
>
> Se acabaron tus noches con su suelta cabellera
> de fogatas . . .
>> "Elegía del Duque de la Mermelada"

In the earlier "Saltimbanqui," however, the fifth stanza, in which the poem returns to the present, discursively tells of the contrast by using a copulative verb followed by the adverbial "hoy":

> Contra la capa blanca del circo, tu figura,
> es hoy . . .
>
> [Against the pale circus tent, today . . .]

This syntax contrasts with how in the more mature "Duque" that pivotal line opens with the adverbial "Ahora," a foregrounding of the temporal motif:

> Ahora, en el molde vistoso de tu casaca
> francesa, . . .
>
> [Now, in the loud design of your French dress-
> coat . . .]

"Duque" exemplifies one among several configurations of the passage/encounter structure highlighted by the way in which Palés used adverbs or adverbials phrases. As we shall see throughout this section, Palés's poems are also built around a variety of other adverbial matrices. Before discussing them specifically, however, it is important to observe three generalizations about them that influence our treatment. First, the adverbial structural matrix consists of contrasting pairs of adverbs. In both "Elegías," for example, the operative dualism is *antes/ahora (ya)*. All use of adverbs in any language, of course, relies on such contrasts (today always assumes an unmentioned yesterday and tomorrow), but stressed here is that Palés poetically foregrounded the adverbs—as he did certain evocative sounds—so that their customary semantic function in discourse is elevated to serve as image. Second, owing to Palés's pattern of metaphorically equating spatial with temporal distance (or telescoping one kind of a distance into another), poems may use more than one pair of adverbials. Third, as illustrated above, the prominent positioning of adverbs is an indicator of Palés's evolving maturity. This positioning therefore also marks the growing importance of the adverbial matrix to the discourse. As the mature discourse is the focus of this analysis, the discussion will be limited to representative poems from *Canciones de la Vida Media* and later.

antes/ahora (ya)

Besides operating in the "Elegías," this dualism is highlighted in the semantic structure of the following poems:

"Canción de la Vida Media"
"Humus"
"Kalahari"
"Mulata-Antilla"
"El Llamado"

"Canción de la Vida Media" opens with the adverbial "Ahora" that ambiguously conveys two ideas: that the "cantar" is commencing and that "Ahora" the poet will sing in a style different from that of another stage in his development: "Ahora vamos de nuevo a canta alma mía; / a cantar sin palabras" ["Now we will sing again, my soul, / sing without words"]. The two meanings of "Ahora" are supported by the adverbial phrase "de nuevo," which simultaneously denotes "again" and connotes that the poet will sing in a new way, making a fresh beginning. The first three stanzas inform us that the poet is now commencing his poem in a new version of an old activity. In the fourth stanza, the contrast between the past and present is reiterated, again employing the adverbial in the dominant position: "Ya eres vieja, alma mía . . ." ["You are already old, my soul"]. The poem's final stanza summarizes the actual state, stressing not any finite activity but, as the rest of the poem confirms, the existential fact of being in a state bent toward infinity. Thus, the poem completes its movement from the implicit *antes* to the "Ahora" and "Ya" to arrive at the prominent "Así estás" in the final stanza: "Así estás, alma mía, en tu grave hora nueva,. . . ." ["So you stand, my soul, at your new grave hour"].

"Humus" employs the *antes/ahora* dualism in a more subdued manner. Not until the third stanza do we learn that "antes" implicitly precedes the poem. Otherwise, the poem focuses on the poet's sense of his interior self, which, as noted in the chapter on the passage structure, also makes the *adentro/afuera* dualism part of this poem's structure. Up from the depths of his soul rises his "sueño y cansancio" in the form of a "Detritus de ideales, de pasiones, de anhelos." The *antes* implicit in the poem was his poetic state of "gran tristeza"; the "ahora" is the emptiness of the world in which he finds himself. The dualism rises to the surface text in the third stanza:

> Antes, rico estanciero,
> en tus zonas azules de poesía,
> y ahora, de tu propia tristeza, pordiosero.

> [Before, a rich rancher,
> on your blue acres of poetry,
> and now, hungry for your own sorrow, a beggar.]

Another poem designed around the dualism *antes/ahora* is "Kalahari." In this poem the speaker reflects upon his answer to the question "¿Por qué ahora la palabra Kalahari?" ["Why now the word Kalahari?"]. At the outset, the emphasis is ambivalent: the speaker not only questions why the word "Kalahari," but why at this moment or time, why in the course of his otherwise Caribbean life this exotic, spontaneous word. Clearly the poem is titled "Kalahari" and the word is the dominant image. On the other hand, the prominence of the adverbial makes us also conscious of the connection between the Caribbean present that Palés is living and the Kalahari desert somewhere in his past, as well as why, at this time in his life (or Puerto Rico's history), "ahora," this word (and thus its evoked image) is haunting him. Observe the first words of the refrain and of the first lines of the stanzas sandwiched between them:

> a. ¿Por qué ahora . . .
>
> b. El día es . . .
>
> c. ¿Por qué ahora . . .
>
> d. Anoche estuve . . .
>
> e. ¿Por qué ahora . . .

    f. Esta mañana . . .

    g. ¿Por qué ahora . . .

    h. Ha surgido de pronto . . .

    i. ¿Por qué ahora . . .

The prominent adverbials in these first lines move the reader back and forth in time. The process begins with the first refrained line in the present, which remains the tense of the entire first stanza. Line d introduces the perfective past from which we return to the present in the refrained line. Line f, still in the perfective, is modified by an adverbial closer in time to the present tense. This movement shifts the focus of the original question from the image "Kalahari" to the experience of having the word crop unexpectedly. The "burdel" was yesterday. This morning he is reading "magazín de cromos."[1] Now, as he looks around at his Caribbean town on a brilliantly clear day, the word "Kalahari" comes to mind. By the end of the poem, the "ahora" we may have read as temporal background to the line weighs considerably more, evoking a broader context: why, not just on this day in the poet's life but at this time in his life.

A similar foregrounding of "ahora" takes place in "Mulata-Antilla," with a few notable differences. Here the specific moment or day is not at issue, so that in the first three stanzas the adverb patently contrasts the present with a time when the poet was blind to the beauty or meaning of the "mulata." As in "Kalahari," in the first three stanzas of "Mulata-Antilla," the effect of the refrain "En ti ahora, mulata" is intended to make the reader conscious of the chronological background to the poem:

> En ti ahora, mulata,
> me acojo al tibio mar de las Antillas.
>
> En ti ahora, mulata,
> cruzo el mar de las islas.
>
> En ti ahora, mulata, . . .
> ¡Oh despertar glorioso de las Antillas!

In the fourth stanza, however, the refrain is substituted by another line:

> Eres ahora, mulata,
> todo el mar y la tierra de las islas.

At that point the chronology of the poet's consciousness begins to diminish in importance and a description of the "Mulatto Woman-Island" remains the focus. Thus, the remaining stanzas simply remain in the present tense and the "ahora" is implied.

The changing function of the adverbial, it should be noted, is another marker of the apparent three stages of writing that this poem underwent. The first three original stanzas, which open with the refrained line, have shorter lines of varying lengths, a tighter rhythmic cadence. The fourth and fifth have consistently longer lines with a looser, flowing rhythm. The sixth and seventh, according to Arce de Vázquez, were appended in the 1950 edition of *Tuntún*.[2] In completing the poem, then, Palés shifted our attention from himself, the emphasis on when *he* began to see the "mulata" differently, to *her* and what he now sees in her. The poem's gradual movement from celebrating Palés's self-consciousness of his accepting and celebrating his true cultural identity to writing a straightforward paean to the *mulata* goddess that symbolizes that identity can be interpreted as an affirmation in the writing of the genuineness of his discourse.

arriba/abajo

In the chapter on Palés' passage structure, we have seen that in "El Pozo" Palés wrote the syntax of certain lines so that "abajo" ("below") is prominently positioned first in its line. We had also seen that the poem differentiates between water's surface imagery evoked by "pozo" and the depths imagery evoked by "en el agua," the *abajo* of the poem. Also in that poem a sense of space is telescoped into a sense of time as the well's depths is later measured in a millenium. In effect, that earlier discussion was about the adverbial configuration of the passage structure and thus allows us to proceed to other examples.

Two other instances of the *arriba/abajo* configuration are "Claro de Luna" and "Boca Arriba." "Clara de Luna" opens with an evocation of a sense of space above, the poet below, and the poet's heart inside. The heart leaps out, looks up to see the moonlight:

> Arriba, por los arboles,
> las aves blandas sueñan,
> y más arriba aún, sobre las nubes,
> recién lavadas brillan las estrellas.

[High, among the treetops,
soft birds dream, and even
higher, above the clouds,
just-washed stars shine still wet.]

After reflecting on the supreme unreality of this hour, the poet's heart leaps again, this time to fly among the stars. In a sense, the frog's leaping out over the grass can be viewed as an application of the *afuera/adentro* dualism which telescopes into the *arriba/abajo*, although the former is not part of the dominant structure.

A poem with the key adverb in the title, "Boca Arriba," discussed in the context of geometric imagery, in Chapter Three, employs the *arriba/abajo* dualism in conjunction with the *afuera/adentro* dualism (to be treated subsequently). In this poem, we recall, the speaker contemplates the night sky above the mountains. His sense of existence is inseparable from his sense of dissolving into the night as he lies under its stars. Above is the amorphous and random mass of night with the Big Dipper's handle picking at the lock of the door into the void. At this point the poem returns to earth. The poet, aware of this circular up and down motion, between the mundane and the celestial, refers to the process as a "gimnasia confusa." In the end, instead of merely returning in a geometric line, the *abajo* implicit in the return telescopes into a metaphorical penetration *adentro*, a word also not explicitly stated, down to his "informe ideación interna":

En la gimnasia confusa,
la informe ideación interna
brota como una medusa
del hueco de una caverna,

y al contacto misceláneo
que la noche desintegra,
se enciende y derrite el cráneo
como una lámpara negra.

[In the dizzying gymnastics,
amorphous internal ideation
sprouts like a medusa
from a cavern's cavity,

and with each random connection
the night disconnects
my skull combusts and melts
like a blackened lantern.]

Then, from an unspecified, remote point comes a "grito." As the stanza informs us, the speaker's central preoccupation is not who or what cried out, rather "¿De dónde?" By now, however, the speaker has become transformed into the dark night so that depths and heights or even geometric points cease to have meaning. The "grito," strictly speaking, came from nowhere, that numinous direction otherwise referred to in other poems as "allá."

afuera/adentro

Three poems with this configuration are "Las Torres Blancas," "Mujer Encinta," and "Los Animales Interiores."

"Las Torres Blancas," discussed in several earlier contexts, opens with a brief allusion to the its "afuera" context in the first line, in which the poet dreams of a distant city. From that mundane point the poem enters the dream world, which includes not only the city but the dream landscape around it. This passage also converts into the *afuera/adentro* context (implicitly conveyed by the word "Sueño") to a sense of *aquí/allá*. Because of this telescoping, the poem like its parallel "Pueblo Negro" might appear to have an *aquí/allá* configuration. This interpretation, however, fails to take into consideration that the sense of distance is a metaphoric sense telescoped from the basic dream-interiority that is the subject of the poem.

In the sonnet "Mujer Encinta," the dualism functions symmetrically in the title, stanza and syntax. The title, for instance, simultaneously describes a woman and her interiority, her child. Each quatrain of the sonnet's octave divides the child-caring woman into an implied *afuera* and *adentro*. In the sestet, the adverbials implied in the quatrains become explicit:

> Afuera dejadez, ademán lento,
> palabra de moroso movimiento,
> en pausa inerte la existencia anclada,
>
> y adentro, Dios, gozoso de armonía,
> pensando y afanando noche y día
> para sacar su mundo de la nada.
>
> [Outside laziness, a slow motion,
> words with a lumbering movement,
> existence anchored in a paralyzed pause,
>
> and inside God, lover of music,
> thinking and planning round the clock
> to midwife his world out of nothingness.]

Similarly, "Los Animales Interiores," a poem discussed at length in a previous chapters, has an *afuera/adentro* configuration. But it does not foreground these adverbials in the manner that the later poems we have discussed although this configuration had been observed earlier in our discussion on the title's emphasizing the animals instead of the medium in which they exist.

(aquí)/allá

The (*aquí*) belongs in parenthesis because its function in the configuration is always implied. From an implied "aquí," referring to the mundane state or merely being in time, the speaker looks out to the undefined and limitless "allá" toward which the poem evokes a sense of traveling. In "Bombo," for instance, the "aquí" is represented by the dance/instrument "bomba." *Aquí* evokes and therefore transports us to "Tombuctú," its cultural origin (*allá*). Once we are transported to that "allá," the ritual dance commences in its mythic timeplace. The second stanza explicitly defines the location of the "allá": "Allá en la jungla de mandinga. . . ." This "Allá" image is also ambiguous. Semantically, it signifies the object of the black tribe's invocation, the numen Bombo. From the vantage point of the speaker (and the reader), "Allá" is an image of the distance from the present to the Timbucktu, the metaphorical jungle from which the numen emerges.

Similar to "Bombo," "Pueblo Negro" is structured to transport the reader to "allá," with no surface mention of "aquí." In it, the "allá" is portrayed as being a distance in the speaker's "brumas interiores," an indication that the (*aquí*)/*allá* dualism is telescoped from the *afuera/adentro* implicit in the town's being "un pueblo de sueño." In "Pueblo Negro," although both dualisms operate simultaneously, the emphasis shifts to (*aquí*)/*allá* as is evident in the poem's description of the woman-song and the lingering sound image (the "ú profunda") in the speaker's soul: what is stressed is the distance across which these surviving evocations travel to the present in the letter "ú." In other words, because the "Pueblo Negro" exists in the soul-interior, like the god Bombo it also emerges from the numinous "allá."

Another example of this dualism operates in "Lagarto Verde." One of those problematic poems with simian imagery, in the first and third stanzas, the Condesito is depicted as directing his guests "por allí, por aquí," adverbs also used for their high-pitched *í*-sound. To evoke a satire of French? To evoke a simian screech?:

> Su alegre rostro de tití
> a todos dice:—Sí.
> —Sí, madame Cafolé, Monsieur Haití,
> por allí, por aquí.
>
> [His happy baby-monkey face
> to everyone says:—*Oui.*
> —*Oui*, Madame Cafaulait, Monsieur Haití,
> This way, that way.]

This image of the refined yet simian Condesito contrasts with the one of him after he hears a green alligator is around:

> Y allá va el Conde de la Limonada,
> con la roja casaca alborotada
> y la fiera quijada
> rígida en epiléptica tensión . . .
> Allá va entre grotescos ademanes,
> multiplicando los orangutanes
> en los espejos de Cristobalón.
>
> [And there goes the Count of Lemonade,
> with his red cossack flaring
> and his savage fallen jaw
> locked in epileptic tension . . .
> There he goes amidst grotesque gestures,
> multiplying orangutangs
> in the mirrors of fat Christophe.]

On the surface level, of course, the repeated "allá" suggests the image of his running off into an unspecified destination. According to Palés's stylistic grammar, however, a resonance of something else is conveyed: that the Count, reacting as he might have in a previous existence, returns to his numen, his origin, the same "farthest shores" to which the Duke of Marmelade will no longer return. That realm, as should be evident by now, exists in no specific direction. In the Palesian vision, the past, present and future are coordinates on a circular journey that can commence from any direction. The spiritual depths and the farthest distances all lead to "allá," the destination that, on the semantic level, renders all the adverbial dualisms identical.

This semantic fusion of adverbials takes place in the surface text of "El Llamado," a culminating poem that employs all the dualisms, a convergence of directions also evoked by the ambiguous title, which simultaneously points to the call from over there and the person here being called. The opening line converts the adverbial into a sound image: "Me llaman desde allá. . . ." The long terminal vowel of "allá" evokes open-ended distance, a place without finality. Then the stanza proceeds to describe the "llamado" as coming from above:

> Por arriba el llamado
> tira de mí con tenue hilo de estrella,
> abajo, el agua en tránsito,
> con sollozo de espuma entre la niebla.
> Ha tiempo oigo la voces
> y descubro las señas.

> [High above the call
> pulls at me with a star's frail line,
> below, the coursing water
> with a sobbing of foam in the fog.
> At times I hear the voices
> and discover the signs.]

The next two stanzas have an *antes/ahora* configuration. The first opens with "Hoy recuerdo: . . ." ["Today I remember: . . ."], then proceeds to describe a memory in the past, setting up the contrast with the following stanza, which opens with "Ahora . . ." Within this *antes/ahora* configuration, the motif of being transported in time, the *(aquí)/allá* dualism reappears. At first the speaker remembers how some time before he was drawn to the call. In the next stanza, he realizes that even as he is present before his love he senses the end of his time on earth is near, and this is described in terms of a physical passage from *aquí* to the *allá* in the black depths of "Ella"'s (the unnamed Filí-Melé's) eyes, that "dulcemente, sin querer" ["sweetly, helplessly"] takes him to her "remoto margen" ["remote shore"].

The stanza that follows employs the *arriba/abajo* dualism to portray the voyage as over a dark sea that inversely parallels the soul-well in "El Pozo." That image was of clear water emitting a blue "fosforescencia" (*fósforo/escencia*). The sea, on the other hand, is black and devoid of the light of poetry. The final stanza, changing the angle of perception, depicts the "Emisario" as returning from the "allá" and reiterates the dilemma of the "llamado," who hears the "llamado." The "Emisario solícito" comes to take him away and he pleads to be left with things that have given him signs of his departure in the previous stanzas: a futile request to thwart an inexorable destiny to voyage "allá."

Phonological Imagery

This hallmark of Palés's style is also the most misunderstood; images that foreground phonological features are immediately associated with the Afro-Antillean poetry. Additionally, the abundance of sound-play in the Afro-Antillean poems has often been taken to mean that the poems are essentially word-play. A closer look at this phonological component of the Palesian style, however, reveals that Palés employed phonological features throughout his work and that he also achieved a complex harmonization of sound-play with the poem's semantic discourse.

Jitanjáfora and Onomatopoetic Devices

Poetry that is generally referred to as *negra* or *negrista* is most often associated with *Jitanjáfora* and onomatopoetic devices. *Jitanjáfora* is the name Alfonso Reyes affixed to the purely phonological image having no semantic function and employed solely for its sound effects. According to José Juan Arrom, the *jitanjáfora* is an act of singing without thinking, a form of mindless ecstasy:

> Sometimes this desire for resonances empties certain words of their meanings, if they had one, in order to leave them simply as sound. And this ultimate singing without thought—a complete suspension of the brain to follow the extasis of the rhythm—is what is called *jitanjáfora* . . . The important thing is the rhythm, the cadence, even though those words don't represent any idea.[3]

A considerable stretch exists between the device Reyes and Arrom identify as the *jitanjáfora* and what critics loosely refer to as *jitanjáfora*, especially in the case of the poetry of Luis Palés Matos. In "La Jitanjáfora en Luis Palés Matos,"[4] for instance, Wáshington Lloréns calls a *jitanjáfra* both the unsemantic and absurdist lines of Dadaist Tristán Tzara—

> Ka tangi te kive
> Kivei
> Ka tangi te moho
> moho

> ka tangi te tike
> ka tangi te tike
> tike

—as well as clearly onomatopoetic devices, such as Luis Lloréns Torres's evocation of the maraca and *güiro* (gourd used as an instrument) in his "El Güiro en A-E-I-O-U":

> Chesque-chesque-chesque-chesque
> y de repente: !¡ches-ches-ches!
> Una maraca macaraca
> dice que qué,
> que qué, que qué,
> y el güiro guicharachero
> quiere que quiere sin querer.
> Relincha el güiro sobre ella:
> ¡Jeje-jéjeje-jejejé!

According to Wáshington Lloréns, the following are also examples of *jitanjáfra* in Palés's poetry:

> Calabó y bambú.
> Bambú y calabó.
> El Gran Cocoroco dice: tu-cu-tú.
> La Gran Cocoroca dice: to-co-tó.
> "Danza Negra"

> ¡Ohé, nené
> ¡Ohé, nené
> Adombe gangá mondé.
> Adombe.
> Candombe del baquiné.
> Candombe.
> "Falsa Canción de Baquiné"

> Ñam-ñam. Africa mastica
> En el silencio—ñam-ñam . . .
> "Ñam-Ñam"

> Sombra blanca en el baquiné
> tiene changó, tiene vodú.
> Cuando pasa por el bembé
> daña el quimbombó, daña el calalú.
> "Lamento"

To the above examples, Lloréns adds the words "Walhalla" and "Kalahari," which he labels "palabra-jitanjáfora" with the latter being an example of "la Jitanjáfora de lo subconsciente." Finally, after citing all these examples, he proceeds to observe that "Luis Palés Matos' *jitanjáfora* is very often onomatopoeia, mere resonances of 'ancestral' instruments" (Lloréns, 5).

This comment contradicts the point of his article that Palés employs *jitanjáfora*, which by definition signifies sounds having no semantic value. Onomatopoeia is not the same as *jitanjáfora*. Although onomatopoeia is a common device throughout Palés's work, contrary to the general belief, at no time does Palés use words for their sound value exclusively; all belong to either the formal or informal lexicon of the Spanish spoken in Puerto Rico, or are sounds that Palés adopts to the semantic system of Spanish. None, in fact, is a *jitanjáfora* in the purest sense of the word, a fact that Lloréns himself also does acknowledge.

"Adombe ganga mondé" may sound just musical but its function is also semantic with variants in various African languages. As Manuel Alvarez Nasario informs us, "ganga" means "men" (from *canga*), denoting a person from the Congo (Alvarez Nasario, 254), and although the original meaning of "mondé" is lost (Alvarez Nasario, 203, n. 95), Palés translates "Adombe ganga mondé" as "Ahora vamos a comer" and "Ahora vamos a bailar" within the poem:

> Ahora comamos carne blanca
> con licencia de su mercé
> Ahora comamos carne blanca . . .

Whether or not Palés's translation is correct, the important thing is that Palés employed this chant for both its phonological and semantic properties.[5]

An extensive treatment of *jitanjáfora* in *poesía negra* is found in Mónica Mansour's *La Poesía Negrista*. Mansour shows how poets who wrote "poesía negrista" discovered or rediscovered the internal rhythm of words. According to her, "Kalahari" is an example of Palés's discovering this kind of rhythm, suggesting by this that the word takes on a phonological life of its own within the context of the poem. (This was also Wáshington Lloréns's point in referring to "Kalahari" as a "palabra-jitanjáfora.") By means of this discovered word, Mansour says, Palés describes "the different feelings or images that a word can evoke, strictly owing to its euphonic sense." (Mansour, 161).

But here Mansour goes too far. Palés treats every word as a word (sound-form, meaning, image). What does it mean to say that the word "Kalahari" takes on a phonological life of its own? Different from true *jitanjáforas,* whose primary function is its sound effect, Palés employs a word such as "Kalahari" for its semantic and historical evocations. As touched upon in our earlier discussion on adverbials, an awareness of time and place is central to Palés's consciousness. In this case, the word is charged with his history, which fills the poet's imagination when he recites the name today. The meaning of "Kalahari" as symbol of history is foregrounded by being set in an uneventful day. And even in the description of that day there is yet other imagery that contrasts with "Kalahari" as temporal image:

> Esta mañana, hojeando un magazín de cromos,
> ante un perrillo de aguas con cinta roja al cuello,
> estuve largo tiempo observando, observando . . .
> No sé por qué mi pensamiento a la deriva
> fondeó en una bahía de claros cocoteros,
> con monos, centenares de monos que trenzaban
> una desordenada cadena de cabriolas.

> ¿Por qué ahora la palabra Kalahari?

> [Leafing through a magazine this morning,
> before a spaniel pup with a red ribbon collar
> I paused a long while staring, staring . . .
> Don't know why, but my rudderless thoughts
> cast anchor in a bay of cameoed palm trees
> with monkeys, monkeys by the hundreds
> braiding a wild crisscross of leaps.

> Why now the word "Kalahari"?]

The ostensibly insignificant "perillo de agua," a dog of Spanish origins ("spaniel pup," etymologically from the Latin for "Spanish"), is an image of the Spanish root in his unconscious. Obviously not a sound image, the Spanish-rooted dog is also juxtaposed to the African desert image that has emerged in the speaker's soul. In sum, although the exotic or euphonic quality of the desert's name might have prompted the poet to repeat "Kalahari," absolutely central to the poem throughout are the images evoked by the word's sense.

Even those examples that come closest to being *jitanjáforas* in Palés's poems are in fact merely instances of onomatopoeia, but not without semantic value. In "Falsa Canción de Baquiné," for instance, a catalog of images make up the line: "—Coquí, cocó,

cucú, cacá—." Coming immediately after the line "Y a la Guinea
su zombí vuelva . . ." ["And let his zombi return to Guinea . . ."],
the line is intended to evoke the jungle by means of both the
graphic image and the sounds. None of the words in the sound
catalogue, however, operate solely on a phonological level; none
is a *jitanjáfora*. The "Coquí" is the name of the Puerto Rican tree
frog who makes the same sound as its name; "cocó" is an allomorph of "coco" or coconut, "cucú" is the onomatopoetic name
of the cuckoo bird, as well as baby talk for "butt," and "cacá" is
another stylized accentuation of a common word of the informal
word for excrement, "caca." Should anyone doubt that Palés was
consciously employing "caca" consider that in the same poem
appear the related images "orines de caimán" ("cayman piss")
and "cagarrutas de cabrón" ("goat turds").

From the evidence already presented, then, it should be clear
that to say the Palesian style employs any *jitanjáfora* is to misapply
the term or to apply it very loosely. Palés's sense of sound and
rhythm is indeed rich, but in his hands these elements become
enrichments to, not substitutes for his treatment of words as words,
with a range of puns and ambiguities. Palés wrote keenly conscious of the whole word, all of whose features he employed.
Thus his phonological sense extends beyond the Afro-Antillean
poems, beyond onomatopoeia and into his equally important intentional ambiguities (puns), which will be discussed at length in
this chapter. It is this Palesian sensitivity to the whole word's
serving the poem on the phonological, morphological, syntactic
(rhythmic) and semantic levels that puts a unique stylistic seal on
his work; no gratuitous or simply aesthetic chirping or sound-
making takes place in any of Palés's poem.

With that in mind, Palés's onomatopoetic images should be
appreciated for their fusion of sound and sense. In "Bocetos Im-
presionistas" ("Impressionist Sketches") the "loros tropicales" are
portrayed in their cages "politiqueando." In "Falsa Canción de
Baquiné" the quaint-sounding "JuJú" (from "Todo está dormido, /
JuJú") is an African word for witch doctor or spirit. "Ñam-Ñam,"
as observed earlier, derives from the word common to many African languages and its meaning is the same as "comer." The onomatopoetic "tuntún," even though patently the drumbeat sound,
never leaves Palés's consciousness as a word. Thus he employs a
plural form: "Tuntún de pasa y grifería / y otros parejeros tuntunes." He also invents an adjectival form in the poem "Intermedios del Hombre Blanco" in which the drums are described as
amphibian creatures with "energía tuntuneca."

A grammatical sense underlying the use of words whose entire value to the poem is ostensibly phonological is also found in "Danza Negra." The simplest onomatopoetic words in this poem are those intended to evoke the animal noises of the pig ("pru-pru-prú") and the frog ("cro-cro-cró"), the same onomatopoetic image of the frog's sound in "El Pozo." Besides their obvious sound function, these onomatopoetic words also participate in a system of poetic gender that is introduced in the first stanza and carries over to the rest of the poem. In that first stanza the paired images "calabó" and "bambú" are cast as masculine and feminine images taking part in this mythical dance. Aside from the suggestion of the images themselves (one assumes "calabó" to be a variant of *calabaza* and feminine and "bambú" the obvious phallic image), what grammatically determines gender in this stanza is not the conventional "o" or "a" endings of grammatical Spanish but "ú" (masculine) or "ó" (feminine) terminal sounds that highlight the onomatopoetic resemblance to a drumbeat, the two vowels that evoke depth in Palés's sound system. Hence the "gran Cocoroco" says "tu-cu-tú" and the female answers with "to-co-tó." This gender system remains consistent throughout the poem; the branding iron sun hovers over "Tombuctú" and the feminine "danza negra" is from "Fernando Póo"; the pig grunts "pru-pru-pru" while the frog's sound is "pro-pro-pro".

Again, Palés's use of sound image is never purely *jitanjáfora*, so that even an ostensibly pure sound image has to be under suspicion of conveying or doing something more. In "Danza Negra," for example, the incurable *conceptista* Palés also played with patterns of Puerto Rican popular speech: Afro-Puerto Rican changes *o*-sounds to *u*, while Andalusian Spanish drops the terminal intervocalic *d*. Thus the "Grand Cocoroco" (an onomatopoetic word that already belonged to Spanish, meaning the same as a "High Muckamuck"), semantically says in Afro-Puerto Rican speech "Tucu tú" and the Grand Cocoroca says in *jíbaro* "Toco to'," which on one level depicts the female as hot and lascivious, but on another level is consistent with Palés's glorifying female images (as shall be shown later on) as a regenerative numinous presence. The counterpoint of African and jíbaro Spanish also punctuates the *mulatez* motif in *Tuntún*.

The sound image "tu-cu-tú" is found in another poem in *Tuntún*. In "Lamento," "tu-cu-tú" is used strictly as an onomatopoetic image of dance movement: "Ya no baila su tu-cu-tú / al—*adombe gangá mondé*—" ["No more dancing his *tu-cu-tú* / *to* the '*adombe gangá mondé*"]. In "Candombe," an allomorph, the refrained "tum-cutum," also evokes drumbeat and dance. Its morphological resemblance to "tu-cu-tú" reaffirms that Palés saw drumbeat, dance and chant as synonymous activities. Hence the image of the *saying* "tu-cu-tú" in "Danza Negra" suggests by the rhythm a chanting in the process of dancing. Finally, it should be observed that Palés did not invent this image, as the sound is related to the a word in popular Puerto Rican speech, *tucutucu*, which means a nervous shaking or fear,[6] a word whose sound suggests an African origin although Alvarez Nasario does not mention it. Also, the sound "tucu-tucu," sung to a particular musical rhythm and accompanied by dance movements, is often used in Puerto Rican Spanish to imitate, a capella, music and dance.

Phonological Images: The Foregrounded Vowel

A separate category of onomatopoetic image used by Palés are long, open vowels highlighted to evoke an additional dimension of tonality or mood, or to enrich the poem with phonic density. We had earlier touched upon this technique in the context of Palés's evoking in some poems a dense medium-state through which the poem invites the reader to journey. Compare the importance of the vowel in the word "grave" in the following stanzas (translated in previous chapters):

> que en grave son
> del canto se dan.
> "Danza Negra"

> hacia la ciudad lúcida de graves torres blancas.
> "Las Torres Blancas"

In both instances, the semantic and imagistic contribution of "grave" to the line is vague. Each context suggests possibilities of meaning, but clearly "grave" as modifier of "son" forms an image quite different from "graves torres." In both instances, however, the word foregrounds its sound to evoke a sense of depth, gravity, but of different kinds. In "Danza Negra," "grave" adds phonological texture to "son," an otherwise graphically bland image; in "Las Torres Blancas," "grave" works in conjunction with other foregrounded long-voweled words ("lúcida de graves torres blancas") to add dark tone to an already graphic image. In both cases, Palés exploits the long and open vowel as a phonological texture whose musicality in the line's rhythmic syntax evokes a graphic image. Hence whatever semantic interpretations we may choose to apply to "grave torres blancas," we respond to the word's sound identically in both cases: the rhythm slows, it evokes a density and weight and, reinforcing the poem's discourse, also evokes a suspension of time.

In "Las Torres Blancas," this time-stopping effect of the foregrounded-vowel device appears more than once. Note the effect of "abarca," "fábula" and "alas" (the effect, being impossible to translate, of course), which evokes a lengthening, a distancing:

> No hay relojes, ni horas, ni día, ni semanas:
> el tiempo allí no existe . . . La eternidad abarca
> la vida misteriosa de esta ciudad de fábula,
> donde los siglos mueven sus fugitivas alas.

> [No clocks, no hours, no days, no weeks:
> there time is nonexistent . . . Eternity surrounds
> the mysterious life of this fable city,
> where the centuries beat their fugitive wings.]

Similarly, in the already discussed "Danza Negra," a sense of timelessness is reinforced by the prominent long-vowels. The dance, we are informed, is the "mariyandá," which is said to be a "grave son" with a "ritmo gordo." One of the possible meanings predicates that contained in the "grave son" and the "ritmo gordo" of the "mariyandá" are the soul of the islands and Africa. The phonological effect, however, evokes a sense of density, the texture of the "son" and "ritmo" as a medium in which we can imagine islands poetically evoked or a soul "vibrando."

Another notable instance of Palés's use of the vowels in "Danza Negra" is found in the couplet:

> Rompen los junjunes en furiosa ú.
> Los gongos trepidan con profunda ó.

In these strongly onomatopoetic, drum-like lines, the adjective's long vowels foreground those adjectives, amplifying the subsequent, actually truncated vowels. Recalling that the modifier "profunda" in "Pueblo Negro" was paired with "ú," note that here "profundo" modifies "ó." In fact, in the above couplet the modifiers themselves are of secondary semantic importance. Important instead is their contribution to the arrangement of vowel sounds. In the first line "furiosa" has the "o" in the penultimate syllable, interrupting the sequence that originated with "jun-junes." Adding to this the proximity of the "u"-sound to the "o," the fourth and final "u" reverberates as it is set in relief by the "o" in "furiosa." Likewise in the second line the "u" in "pro-funda" sets in relief the sixth "o" lengthened in that line. Even more effective as synesthesia, the long "u," lengthened by the nasal "n," evokes a graphic image of depth that is reinforced by the meaning of "profunda." A different but parallel combination of sound and sense works with "furiosa," as the juxtaposing of the modifier's stronger array of vowels and consonants in "furi-osa" beside the simple "ú" foregrounds an onomatopoetic effect of fury.

Of the phonological devices in Palés style, then, we can arrive at three conclusions. First, the prominent "o," "u," and "a" were used to evoke slowness, density, depth, and distance. Second, that onomatopoetic images belong to a subset of the fore-grounded-vowel device and thus one of the functions of the drum-sounding onomatopoetic (and rhythm) is also intended to evoke slowness, density, depth, etc. Third, that while the drum-beat effect is peculiar to the poems in *Tuntún*, the foregrounded-vowel device is present in both Afro-Antillean and non-Afro-Antillean poems. An example that confirms the uniformity of this device in Palés's work is "Nocturno" (cited and translated in an earlier chapter), a non-Afro-Antillean poem that evokes an image of the night as water, a dense medium in which a "drop" of night percusses as if against a large drum. The drop/drum effect is achieved through the foregrounding of vowel sounds.

In conclusion, Palés identified the sound of the vowel with the timelessness with which he was obsessed, whether as dream, numen, or *allá*. But the result was a contradiction of purposes. For although Palés was, on the one hand, a *conceptista* and highly verbal in his style, his poems also bespeak of a consistent mini-malist movement toward an essential sound, the creation of the ultimate poem, not unlike the idea he shared with José I. De Diego Padró in their youth: to write a wordless song.

Metaphors

Como-simile

Palés's *como*-similes reiterates his consciousness operating on two levels: mundane-spiritual, physical-metaphysical, body-soul, interiority-exteriority, surface-depth. This *como*-simile is most frequently used in the first person poems from *Azaleas* (1917) to the unpublished *Canciones de la Vida Media* (1925), books in which Palés employed an average of sixteen *como*-similes per book. The sonnet "Neurosis," for instance, in attempting to explain this dualism unsurprisingly resorts to the simile five times, more than any other in *Azaleas*. By contrast, in *Tuntún* only four poems employ a *como*-simile, a pace sustained in his later poems (1954–57), in which we find a total of three.

Understanding that the simile is a weaker metaphor, and more likely to appear more frequently among a poet's earlier work, one must also add that for some poetic styles the simile abounds even in poetic maturity. Palés's virtuosity at metaphor making would put him in that category. But in his case the diminishing number of *como*-similes in later poems also parallels the evolution of Palés's spiritual consciousness. He started out with a Western metaphysical view, characterized by the Aristotelian principles of body and soul as separate. In the most mature poems, however, Palés's celebrates the animism or spiritualism of the numen. Accordingly, this changed consciousness is reflected in the diminishing occurrences of *como*-simile. On the other hand, the *como*-similes he does use consistently wed the material and immaterial into a single image, a symbolic fusion of the physical and the ideational. To illustrate, the syntactic transformation of the simile of the night "como un pozo infinito" in "Voces del Mar" accounts for the water metaphor of night in "Nocturno" and later the "gotear soñoliento" that telescopes into the "tamboriles" in "Elegía del Duque de la Mermelada." In other words, with respect to such recurring images, the more transparent *como*-similes simply serve as glosses to the deep semantic structure of later metaphorical transformations. In performing this function, the *como*-simile is a stylistic indicator of an earlier stage of Palés's spiritual consciousness.

The important differences of spiritual vision in early and mature stages is one reason why over the years critics and readers have felt the need to categorize poems as "white" and "black." In this loose sense they are: Palés in his maturity had consciously adopted a non-Western (his own and not necessarily African) vision. The mistake was in believing that, because the "black" poems switched to a non-Western notion of the spiritual, that his conversion was temporary and that Palés had been evoking that exotic African spirituality as a literary device. In fact, Palés had genuinely evolved to that stage.

Composite Metaphors

Composite metaphors in Spanish consist of a form image (N_1) that lends its form to a secondary image of substance or matter (N_2), e.g., "pueblo de sueño." Palés used them frequently in patterns that permits our dividing them into four groups. In group A belong images of countable forms that consist of uncountable matter (in which terms like "sueño" and "pesadilla" are used in the sense of *dreamstuff* and not instances or countable experiences):

A:
(N_1 *de* N_2)

tortuga de plata
trampa de polvo azul
botonazo de luz
catedral de ceniza
arbol de niebla
pueblo de sueño
ciudad de sueño
gándaras de sueño
campos de pesadilla
arrabales de sombra
dedos de bronce y sombra

In group B belong images of countable forms consisting of countable matter:

B:
(N_1 *de* N_2)

racimos de cantos
faldón de cañas
rumba de llamas

In group C belong images of uncountable forms consisting of uncountable matter:

C:
(N₁ *de* N₂)

atmósfera de dicha
claror de agonía

In group D belong images of uncountable forms consisting of countable matter:

D:
(N₁ *de* N₂)

dulzura de merengues y caratos
horchata de salmos

Except in the case of C, there is a fusion of masslessness and form, of concreteness and immateriality.

Representing the sharpest contrast of these features, the group of most interest to this discussion is A. It comprises the greatest number of microcosmic examples of Palés's intention to concretize the ephemeral. In group A, the countable form image is concrete and physical, evoking a distinct form but not appealing to the sense in any foregrounded way, while the matter image is unconcrete, formless and sensorial. Owing to these sets of features, the composite metaphor evokes an image of something that is non-material yet has form. A similar operation takes place in varying degrees, and highlighting other semantic features, in the other three groupings. In group B (in which "cantos" is not concrete yet physical in a sensorial way), concrete images are melted down to take the form of the form image. In group C, the composite features of "atmósfera de dicha" and "claror de agonía" evoke an image of something unconcrete and formless yet made physical by being perceived by the senses. In D, the physically formed sense of the matter image is dissolved into the formlessness of the "form" image. In all groups, the dynamic reiterates the Palesian obsession with making the ineffable palpable or an essence of something physical reach us through the senses. In other words, these composite images are variations on the continuous activity of the supreme unconcrete, unphysical essence, Filí-Melé (as will be discussed in the next chapter), whose body is the poem that invokes her.

Synesthetic metaphors

Some examples of the composite image also illustrate Palés's use of synesthetic metaphor, or the association of an image usu-

ally perceived by one of the senses with an image perceived by
another of the senses. A few of the examples of composite metaphors were also synesthetic. The image "racimos de cantos" is
derived from a metaphorical comparison of a visual image ("racimos," "bunch,") with a sound image ("cantos," "songs"). In
"Pueblo Negro" the "atmósfera de dicha" of the earlier discussion
is actually part of a metaphor comparing the woman's "canto
sensual" to "una clara atmósfera de dicha." That same "canto" is
also said to contain the "ú" that is heard after the poem ends.
This information, however, is conveyed in a synesthetic image
that associates the "u"-sound with its graphic image, which in
turn telescopes into a metaphor of a womb.

In brief, in addition to the previously discussed sense-
associated N de N imagery, Palés's poems frequently evoke the
stimulus to one of the senses by images that stimulate another
of the senses, a device that attunes our sense to the irrational.
Thus the sun becomes a cup of wine ("Este Olor a Brea," "This
Smell of Tar"), the black race surges and swells ("Danza Negra"),
the black man drinks "his sorrow cold" ("Preludio en Boricua,"
"Prelude in Boricua").

Symbol and Allegory

Allegory is the least frequently used metaphorical device in
Palés's style. In "Lamento" the white man as symbol of white
culture is depicted as a malevolent "sombra blanca." Also, in "El
Menú" the title serves as an allegorical image of the exploited
Caribbean that spreads out in a feast for the "peregrino." More
frequent are the instances of symbol. "Don Quijote" represents
Spain in "Canción Festiva" as does the "pirata" in "Ten con Ten."
The phallic "Gallo" is a male symbol of Antillean sensuality and
has its counterpart in "Mulata-Antilla," Sinclair Lewis's "Babitt"
symbolizes Anglo America, and the "Duque de la Mermelada,"
the colonized capitulation to Western culture. Also, the anthropomorphic images of the numina are metaphors that operate as well
as symbols. Tembandumba, Bombo and the singing black woman
symbolize African numinous origins just as Don Quijote does
Spain. Also God, who symbolizes the West, and the ñáñigo, symbol of the African descendant, become participants in a symbolic
act that images the spiritual *mestizaje* that forms the Antillean
numen.

Telescoping

Telescoping is that device by which one element of a metaphorical comparison is compared with a third element thus chaining

images in a complex metaphor. In "Canción de la Vida Media," which has been cited several times, the speaker's "alma" is first compared to a tree. At the end of the poem, however, the erectness and pointedness of the tree is compared to a vessel pointing skyward toward the deep night (numinous water metaphor in the Palesian lexicon). Similarly, in its final stanza "San Sabás" is first metaphorically referred to a "peñon" ("rocky mountain") and then, is compared to a vessel pointing skyward (like the tree in "Canción"):

>Rugía el viento en las arenas,
>aullaba en la sombra el chacal,
>pero en el fondo de la noche
>se erguía el peñón colosal
>recto, profundo y luminoso
>como una proa espiritual.
>
>[Wind bellowed over the sands,
>howled in the jackal's shadow,
>but into night's fathoms
>towered the colossal rock
>erect, lunging, luminous,
>like a spiritual prow.]

This telescoping device is important in virtually all of Palés's poems. In the Filí-Melé cycle, notably in those poems in which the "Filí-Melé" appears in the surface text, "Puerta al Tiempo en Tres Voces" and "La Búsqueda Asesina," the protean nature of this woman-essence can only be shown through a constant telescoping. Hence in "Puerta al Tiempo en Tres Voces" the first image of Filí-Melé as a tree telescopes into a disappearing being who then becomes a sailing vessel, the vessel for his numinous journey. In "La Búsqueda Asesina" as well, the telescoping device evokes a sense of Filí-Melé's constant changes of time, place and states of matter. This device and these poems will be discussed in greater detail in the following chapter devoted to the Filí-Melé cycle.

Puns

One of the reasons why Palés's antipoetic qualities have been misperceived is due in great measure to the critics' overlooking the importance of the pun in Palés's technical repertory. Palés makes use of punning ambiguity in three ways. The first plays with the semantic features of words. One of the most elaborate examples of this kind appears in "Canción Festiva" (the italics are mine):

> ¿En qué *lorito aprendiste*
> ese patuá de melaza,
> Guadalupe de mis trópicos,
> *mi suculenta tinaja?*
> *A la francesa, resbalo,*
> sobre tu *carne mulata,*
> que a falta de pan, tu *torta*
> es prieta *gloria* Antillana.

Here is a possible straightforward translation:

> In what little parrot did you grasp
> that molasses patois,
> Guadalupe of my tropics,
> my succulent pottage.
> Impetuously I slide,
> over your mulatto flesh,
> as lacking bread, your cake
> is a dark Antillean delight.

The stanza portrays the island of Guadalupe as an Antillean *mulata*. The first line uses two puns: the first, the diminutive "lorito," plays with the ambiguity of two senses of "loro," parrot and mulatto. The second line plays with "aprendiste." One sense of the word is literally to learn: "¿/En qué lorito aprendiste a hablar ese patuá de melaza?" The second sense plays with the etymological root *aprehender,* thus evoking the history of apprehending the language by apprehending (marrying?) the *loro,* mulatto or apprehending (catching) the parrot. Also in that stanza, the "patuá" has the modifier "de melaza," whose phonological effect evokes the sweet and slippery quality of one of the word's meanings, molasses. The word "melaza," however, is derived from the Greek prefix *melas* for the color black. From this Palés squeezes out the meaning *melas* + *-aza* suggesting a multitude of blackness. In the fourth line, "mi suculenta tinaja" is a metaphor that compares of the Guadalupe-mulatta to a Caribbean pottage, or "tinaja." This meaning of "tinaja" describes her as edible, alluding to her savoriness, especially in oral sex, as the subsequent lines bear out. But "tinaja" also evokes the wide, round clay pot used for cooking the stew, thus rendering an image of her "succulent" physical form (to popular Caribbean male tastes, thin is less attractive), an amorous syntesthic image that also performs in "Ten con Ten" using the same "tinaja":

> Podrías lucir, esbelta,
> sobriedad de línea clásica,
> si tu sol, a fuerza de oro,
> no madurase tus ánforas
> dilatando tus contornos
> en amplitud de tinaja.

> [You could have shone, tall,
> a classically-lined sobriety,
> if your sun's gold force
> hadn't ripened your amphora thighs
> amplifying their slenderness
> wide as earthen jars.]

Returning to the quoted stanza from "Canción Festiva para Ser Llorada," "A la francesa" evokes the stereotype of the French as lovers as well as their fondness of good food. But the phrase also signifies *impulsivamente*. This connotative meaning is reinforced by the word "resbalo," which suggests both a physical and moral sliding. The speaker thus acknowledged the physical indulgence of sliding over her "carne mulata" as an impulsive act. The "carne mulata" plays with the double meanings of "carne" as both meat and flesh. Thus, the "carne mulata" (which suggests a kind of preparation of meat) refers to both the meat in stew and the mulatta's flesh. And the region of her flesh toward which the speaker has been working is her genitalia, which appears in a culinary pun. The poet could survive on her "carne mulata" because, lacking bread, the food for life, her "torta" is enough. "Torta," of course, signifies "loaf" or "cake," but as well popularly denotes a woman's genitalia. Lastly, the praise given to her "torta" also plays with puns. The word "gloria" is itself a term denoting a kind of cake.

Of course numerous other, less elaborate semantic puns operate through Palés's work. In "Canción Festiva," the Haitian runaway slave Macandal is described as hiding "por la profunda maraña" ["in the thicket"], although "maraña" also refers to kinky hair and thus the thicket of slaves' hair. Thus "maraña" can also serve as an image of head or mind, in which the numinous Macandal "bate su gongo" ["beat his drum"] inspiriting his revolution. In "Lagarto Verde," the Condesito de la Limonada is described as a "monada," a word that means both the act or gesture of a monkey as well as a cute act or one of affectation.

A second kind of ambiguity plays with the morphology of words. In the above stanza from "Canción Festiva," which was used to illustrate semantic ambiguities, the final word "Antillana" is a morphological pun: the wide-hipped mulatta is obviously "Anti-llana" ["anti-flat"]. In the early poem "Tic-Tac," which he later incorporates into "Voz de lo Sedentario y lo Monótono," Palés syllabifies the word "interminable" in a way that creates an ambiguity: "inter-/minable." Broken up in this way, "interminable" functions in two ways: *interminable* as signifying unending and as a suffixed form of *minar, inter-minable*, an early play on Palés's sense of an endless medium.

Similarly, in "A Luis Lloréns Torres" the root word "fundo" is made to rhyme with "profundo", i.e., favoring the "fundo" as Lloréns is pictured in that poem:

> Corriste a su llamada y abandonaste el fundo
> que fue para tu numen telúrico y profundo . . .
>
> [You ran to its call and abandoned the country place
> that was for your soul, teluric and profound . . .]

Lastly, as discussed in the chapter 1 and in examples above, in "El Menú" the reference to Rubén Darío's dedicating "un opúsculo" to the Antillean pines is also a morphological pun. The sarcastic tone of the poem encourages one to consider that here "opúsculo" can be read as either one word or two.

A third kind of pun in Palés's style is the ambiguous syntax. The opening lines of "Las Torres Blancas" illustrate:

> Sueño, bajo la comba de noche estrellada,
> con una ciudad llena de graves torres blancas.

These lines may be understood in two ways: as either a declarative right-branching sentence ("Sueño con . . .") or as a long noun phrase *prednom* in which "Sueño" is a noun and the phrases that follow are modifiers. As a declarative sentence the description of the "ciudad" resembles a landscape portrait, although the ambiguity of "Sueño" serves throughout to reiterate the borderline dreamstate of the poem: is the poem a depiction of a dream or a recounting the act of dreaming? The final lines explicitly introduce the dreamer ("Yo anhelo . . .") and resolves the ambiguity and returns us to the certainty of the mundane state.

In "Pueblo Negro," the following couplet is intentionally ambiguous:

> Alguien disuelve perezosamente
> un canto monorrítmico en el viento.

> [Someone lazily dissolves in the wind
> a monorhythmic song.]

"Alguien" literally "disuelve," the ambiguous syntax is suggesting, "en el viento [como] un canto monorrítmico." Moreover, as earlier observed in the detailed discussion of this poem in chapter 2, the ambiguity hinges on a popular, *boricua* meaning of "canto": her "piece" or "cunt" and the poet's making her "canto" and her "vida" synonymous. The song has ceased to be a mere song, having become synonymous with the woman and the "negra" eventually evolves to embody a sexually-charged musical presence encapsuled in the image of her "canto sensual." This baroque conceit built upon an initial syntactic ambiguity in "Pueblo Negro" produces a woman image that is consistent with the woman metaphors analyzed further ahead in this chapter. As will be shown in greater detail in that discussion, "la negra," with her spreading song, aroma and sensuality, prefigured the sensual Mulata-Antilla who embodies the numen of the Caribbean, and ultimately serves as the model for Palés's image of the amorphous, ephemeral essence of poetry, Filí-Melé, in "Puerta al Tiempo en Tres Voces."

That poem also provides an example of an ambiguous syntax:

> Y ahora ¿a qué trasmundo, perseguida
> serás, si es que eres?

> [And now, to what world beyond, will you be
> pursued, if you are?]

Placed at the end of the question, the "si es que eres" clause has two possible meanings. One inquires whether Filí-Melé exists and the other whether she is "perseguida." This ambiguity echoes the two uncertainties expressed throughout the poem: the existence of the fleeting numen and whether the speaker will ever attain her. Any doubt over whether this ambiguity is intentional is resolved in the opening lines of section 3 which, by defining the status of speaker and love object, respectively *yo* and *tú* in a

compound sentence, explicitly answer the two questions raised
in the above ambiguity:

> Pienso, Filí-Melé, que en el buscarte
> te estoy encontrando,
> y te vuelvo a perder en el oleaje
> donde a cincel de espuma te has formado.

> [I believe, Filí-Melé, that in seeking you
> I an encountering you,
> but again I lose you in wave after wave
> where you've sculpted yourself with a chisel of foam.]

Animal Metaphors

Animal imagery makes up a veritable zoo in Palés's poetry and
usually serve to compare an animal's physical features with some
human characteristics. "El Gallo" ["The Rooster"] celebrates the
Caribbean's symbol of sexual potency. Bees are implied to swarm
in a hive that is Filí-Melé's hair. From that zoo, however, certain
major animal metaphors recur most and are central to appreciating Palés's style.

The first is the bovine metaphor, which can be either an ox
or a cow. In the early poem "Los Ocios Pluviales" ["The Rainy
Pastimes"], we see both male and female bovine imagery, although the "buey" ["ox"], strictly speaking, is used as metaphor
of a desire in his spirit:

> ¡Oh esta tarde de vacas color rosa
> me despierta un buey manso en el espiritú,
> y en una metempsicosis azul
> me pone a comer yerba con las vacas!

> [Oh on this afternoon of rose-colored cows
> a gentle ox awakes me in my soul,
> and in a blue transmigration of spirits
> puts me out to graze among the cows!]

The poem ends with the same metaphor:

> Rabí Jeschona, blanco nazareno,
> yo soy buey manso y rubio . . .

[Rabbi Jeschona, white Nazarene,
I am a blond, gentle ox . . .]

The same "buey" metaphor, discussed and cited in another, earlier context, is used to describe the "mansedumbre" of the sailors
in "Fantasías de la Tarde."

The feminine bovine image used as *metaphor* differs from the
"buey" in that the cow image is subdued so the word *vaca* never
appears in the surface text. In "¡Ay, Se Fue la Aldeana!" we recall,
the country girl is said to have eyes in which innocence grazes
"bovinamente." But this bovine metaphor also intends to describe
the rest of her:

> cuyos cabellos huelen a albahaca,
> y cuya carne toda cría un vaho
> íntimo de pesebre y hortaliza.

> [whose hair smells of sweet basil,
> and whose flesh breeds all over
> a private odor of manger and farm.]

This bovine metaphor parallels its transformation in "Pueblo
Negro":

> la negra de las zonas soleadas
> que huele a tierra, a salvajina, a sexo.

> [the black woman from sunbaked zones,
> who smells of earth, of game, of sex.]

Here, although the bovine metaphor might seem remote, the similarities are found on the semantic level. Where the "aldeana" is
expressly bovine, the black woman is compared to an "animal
doméstico." But both images describe the secretion of body odor
and both odors evoke bestial images as well as pack a sexual
charge. The major difference is that the "aldeana" evokes innocence, while the black woman evokes experience. Note how the
sexual reference to the "aldeana cuya carne toda cría un vajo /
íntimo . . ." is poetic compared to the antipoetic "huele a tierra,
a salvajina, a sexo." In both these poems, in which the black and
white women are depicted according to Western conventions,
Palés would appear to not challenge Western stereotypes. On the
other hand, he does break with convention in depicting the black
woman as a mythic source in his language and his culture. Quite

aware of the aforementioned conventions regarding the depiction
of women, to illustrate, he used them in "Ten con Ten" to portray
Puerto Rico as a composite of the stereotypes associated with
each race:

> Pasarías ante el mundo
> por civil y ciudadana,
> si tu axila—flor de sombra—
> no difundiera en las plazas
> el rugiente cebollín
> que sofríen tus entrañas.

> [You could have passed before the world
> for cultured and civilized,
> if your armpits—flowers of shadow—
> didn't spread through the plazas
> the pungent odor of onions
> your entrails lightly fry.]

The most controversial metaphors in Palés's zoo are, of course,
the simian metaphors. Different from the bovine imagery, the
semantic function of the simian metaphor varies from poem to
poem. In "Lagarto Verde" and "Elegía del Duque de la Mermelada," for example, the satirizing of their character's colonial ways
is intended to be punctuated by the convention of the mimicking
ape. Mimicking European culture is also what the Antillean aristocracy in general (both white and black) does and thus is also
depicted as "una aristocracia macaca" in "Preludio en Boricua."
On the other hand, the simian image has also conventionally
been a verbal weapon of racists. So in the context of Palés's celebration of Caribbean roots, and specifically its enrichment by its
African numen, the significance of his use of simian metaphors
can shift with the reader's interpretation. Palés, however ad-
vanced in his cultural perspectives, doubtless harbored certain
contemporaneous attitudes that he employed to explode, but
therefore did ambiguously celebrate.

Besides those examples of simian metaphors already shown, in
"Canción Festiva para Ser Llorada," for example, the
anthropomorphically-described smaller Antillean islands are
compared to playful "titís" or monkeys. Whether this simian
metaphor is intended to image the inhabitants of those islands is
subject to interpretation. In the case of St. Kitts, for example, the
complete image employs an "ovillo de viento" ["a spool of
wind"], meaning the hurricane, with which the "titís" play. Re-

garding St. Thomas, on the other hand, the explicitly stated inhabitants are referred to as "los negros." Santo Domingo is also
portrayed in simian imagery:

> Para cuidarme el jardín
> con Santo Domingo basta.
> Su perenne do de pecho
> pone intrusos a distancia.
> Su agrio gesto de primate
> en lira azul azucara,
> cuando borda madrigales
> con dedos de butifarra.

> [To look after my garden
> Santo Domingo will do.
> His perennial tenor note
> keeps intruders at bay.
> His sour primate grimace
> sweetens into blue poetry
> when he embroiders madrigals
> with fingers like Catalan sausages.]

This is also another illustration of Palés's use of ambiguous syntax. One reading suggests we read the primate image as a reference to deceptive appearances: "[what appears to be] his bitter
primate grimace. . . . " is sweetened when he sings. But note
that the reflexive *se* is missing and *azucar* is transitive but has no
direct object. Thus another reading, the grammatical one, informs
us that when he sings he charms anyone. Lastly, however, owing
to the absence of the reflexive pronoun, the syntax also offers a
baroque pun, so another reading of the line renders the verse "en
lira azula su cara" ["in poetry blues his face"], which on the
one hand elaborates the primate image and, on the other hand,
neutralizes the racist nuances of the primate image. Again, Palés
seems to brazenly use the white mind's idea of the black for its
shock effect only to proceed and contradict that image, also for
its shock effect. This interpretation is supported by his sustained
anti-Westernism in "Canción Festiva para Ser Llorada" and other
poems in *Tuntún*, as observed in previous contexts. In sum, from
playing with racist fire, Palés occasionally gets burned in saying
racist-sounding things, a contradiction that, wittingly or unwittingly, captures the *afroantillanismo* of the white *boricua*.

Lastly, among the animal metaphors the frog and toad offer a
rich source of imagistic associations which, as has been shown

throughout this study, Palés exploits in diverse ways. The "alcalde" in "Pueblo," is portrayed as a subdued frog or toad "chapoteando" over the water of his life; the drums are depicted as
amphibian creatures in "Intermedios del Hombre Blanco." In the
first example the implied paunchiness of the mayor is compared
to that of the toad; in the second, the drumbeats are compared
to a rhythmic croaking. In another poem, however, other frog-
like features are used. "La Hora Propicia," in which the poet
describes his desire for a girl he had watched grow into woman-
hood, compares the poet's eyes to leaping toads:

> Mis ojos avarientos
> como dos sapos miopes,
> saltando diariamente a su riqueza . . .
>
> [My covetous eyes
> like two myopic toads,
> daily leaping to her wealth . . .]

A variant of the leaping toad image also operates in "Claro de
Luna," which compares the heart to a leaping frog:

> En la noche de luna, esta noche
> de luna clara y tersa,
> mi corazón como una rana oscura
> salta sobre la hierba.
>
> [In the moonlit night, this night
> with a clear, terse moon,
> my heart like a dark frog
> leaps on the grass.]

Because virtually every instance of the frog/toad metaphor is
accompanied by the numinous water image, this discussion can
be shortened by referring the reader to the chapter 5, "Images of
the Numen." One notable exception from that group of numinous
water images is found in "El Pozo," in which yet another physical
feature of the frog is foregrounded: its prehistoric reptilian appearance. Its physical appearance symbolizes a confluence of diachrony and synchrony since, evoking a prehistoric age, it lives
simultaneously in both numinous past and mundane present.

Woman Metaphors

In Palés's post-1920 poetry, the woman image serves as a mimetic representation of a real woman in only two poems: "Can-

ción Festiva" and "¡Ay Se Fue la Fue la Aldeana!" In the latter, she is the "aldeana," of course; in "Canción Festiva," she is the female Cuban speaker in the one-stanza monologue: "Me voy al titiringó / de la calle de la prángana. . . ."

Although this voice and the "aldeana" differ from the mythic black woman in "Pueblo Negro," note that Palés ascribes to the three a sudoriferous quality. This device, a variant of which is his association of woman with a sexual redolence, is employed to paint the black woman as dissolving into a sensually redolent song. And, as in that example, this device also shows how in his mature poems Palés's woman images literally dissolve into myth, the pattern of the major woman images in Palés's post-1920 poems.

The most frequently recurring woman-myth metaphor of this later period is a dancer. In "Las Torres Blancas," the woman is a being whose body emits "azules llamas" ("blue flames") and whose gait has the rhythm of a poem. In "Majestad Negra," Tembandumba symbolizes the African numen incarnate in the rumba, *macumba, candombe, and bámbula* danced in the Caribbean. In "Ten con Ten," Puerto Rico is the "bayadere" who dances "un ten con ten" ["a neither this nor that"].

From these dancing-woman images emerges the "Mulata-Antilla" ("Mulatto Woman-Island"). Like the earlier Diosa-Poesía, the mulatta's being is in perpetual dance. And, as with the black woman in "Pueblo Negro," who became a spiritual presence, the "mulata" is simultaneously the color and tone of the entire Caribbean in which the speaker is submerged:

> Eres ahora, mulata,
> todo el mar y la tierra de mis islas.
> Sinfonía frutal cuya escalas
> rompen furiosamente en tu catinga.
> He aquí en su verde traje la guánabana
> con sus finas y blandas pantaletas
> de muselina; he aquí el caimito
> con su leche infantil; he aquí la piña
> con su corona de soprano . . . Todos
> los frutos ¡oh mulata! tú me brindas,
> en la clara bahía de tu cuerpo
> por los soles del trópico bruñida.
>
> [Now you are, mulatto woman,
> all the lands and sea of my islands.
> A symphony of fruit whose scales

furiously overture in your sweat.
Here the green-dressed sour sop,
with her fine, white muslin bloomers;
the *caimito* full of baby's milk;
here the pineapple crowned
like a soprano . . . Every fruit,
Oh mulatto woman, you offer me,
in the bright bay of your body
burnished by the tropic's suns.]

In "Plena del Menéalo" ("Shake It *Plena*"), a dancing woman imagistically embodies Puerto Rico:

Bochinche de viento y agua . . .
sobre el mar
está la Antilla bailando
—de aquí payá, de ayá pacá—
menéalo, menéalo
en el huracán.

[Rumoring of wind and water . . .
On the sea
the Island is dancing
—back and forth, side to side—
shake it, shake it
in the hurricane.]

The symbolic *mulata*-Puerto Rico in "Plena del Menéalo" dances the same dances that, in "Majestad Negra," invoked the African goddess Tembandumba:

Ay, cómo zumba tu zumbo
—huracanada balumba—
cuando vas tumbo en tumbo
bomba, candombe, macumba . . .

[Ay, how your booming cabooms
—hurricane-force mass—
when sway on sway you move
bomba, candombe, macumba . . .]

In both "Majestad Negra" and "Plena del Menéalo," however, the dance represents something more than the *mulata's* sensuality. The dance, as seen above, invokes the African numen contributing one of the "potencias expansivas" mentioned in "Mulata-Antilla." That sensual spirit (according to Palés) liberates her

twice, in her sexuality as woman and, as symbol, politically dis-
qualifying and thus sparing the Antilles from being absorbed by
"Babbitt Máximo":

> porque eres, mulata de los trópicos,
> la libertad cantando en mis Antillas.

> [because you are, mulatto woman of the tropics,
> liberty singing in the Islands.]
> > "Mulatto Woman-Island"

> Mientras bailes, no hay quien pueda
> cambiarte el alma y la sal.
> Ni agapitos por aquí,
> ni místeres por allá.

> [While you dance, none exists
> who can change your soul and salt.
> Niether *Agapitos* from down here,
> nor Misters from up there.]
> > "Plena del Menéalo"[7]

All the poems cited above also show that Palés's woman images
are also love objects, which he turned into metaphors, a dominant
feature in his mature poems post-1920. For this reason, in the
pre-1920's woman images, among which do appear some women
images intended to mimetically represent real women ("Guay-
amesa" "Esa Mujer" and "Pero Ahora, Mujer"), we come across
prefigurations of later female metaphors. In "Dans la Nuit," for
example, the "princesa bella" is his earliest *modernista* prefiguration of the woman-poetic essence. Also, "La Danza de las Horas"
("Dance of the Hours") employs a metaphor that prefigures the
dancing *mulata* in a number of later poems. And, in a second
version of "Tic-Tac," part of which is later incorporated in "Voz
de lo Sedentario y lo Monótono," from the "ciudad dormida"
emerges "Ella," who prefigures the Diosa-Posía and (the Diosa
herself being a prefiguration) Filí-Melé, who as an image of the
essence of poetry epitomized the Palesian woman metaphor. For,
in a culmination of his poetic self-consciousness, his Filí-Melé
embodies the conversion of all aspects of the numinous and procreative in Palés's vision of woman. She is the poem and all creativity, mother and woman.

7

The Numinous Site: The "Filí-Melé" Cycle

Palés's later poems have never received the critical or popular attention that they deserve. This neglect is largely owing to the attention paid to *Tuntún de Pasa y Grifería*, but has resulted as well from the fact that his reputation was founded on his writing *poesía negra*, a context in which the later poems becomes ostensibly strange and ungermane. In them, Palés returned to traditional poetic forms and, at times, to his earlier lyrical voice. Also, they reflect on his life as a poet. Nevertheless, despite appearances, the later poems also contain vestiges of his antipoetic, Afro-Antillean work. One way of interpreting these late poems is as a separation of heretofore interwoven personas. If the pre-Afro-Antillean and the Afro-Antillean poems alternated between being about language and about an underlying numinous quality in the world and language, the later poems could be described as efforts to purify, to write a *pure* poetry. (This effort is quite possibly the influence of the Puerto Rican academic poetry scene, which was highly affected by the "pure poetry" tenets of Spanish Nobel Laureate and island resident, Juan Ramón Jiménez.)

Palés's last poems, then, are about the creative essence of poetry, a discourse that is reminiscent of or possibly influenced by Heidegger. Jaime Benítez, the former president of the University of Puerto Rico, a friend and admirer and sometime patron of the poet (via university residencies), touched upon that discourse in his introduction to the "Homenaje a Luis Palés Matos" issue of the university's literary journal *La Torre*.[1] After quoting from Heidegger's essay on Hölderlin, Benítez affirmed that "Palés Matos is going to say the same as Heidegger, not from frequent visits with the German philosopher, rather by intimate flashes of brilliance in which intuition becomes metaphysics."[2] Coming upon Benítez's comment was encouraging indeed, although it was discouraging that in the entire *Homenaje,* none of the scholarly contributors picked up on the philosophical theme.

Palés began writing the two specifically "Filí-Melé" poems, according to Arce, in 1949. His earlier sonnets in the cycle were presumably written in the forties. Heidegger's *Being and Time* was published in German in 1927 and may well have been translated into Spanish by the early 1940's. In fact, Benítez's belief that Palés merely coincided with Heidegger is contradicted by the poet Juan Antonio Corretjer, who also knew Palés well and confirmed that "Palés was an avid reader; he read little poetry, many novels, a lot of philosophy."[3] In sum, owing to the exact coincidences in imagery and Corretjer's comments, that Palés did read the German philosopher seems highly probable. Heidegger would appear to have provided the poet with a philosophical framework in which to verbalize Palés's already demonstrated conviction in the need to explore non-Western answers to basic questions asked by religion and philosophy.

Heidegger differentiated between Being-in-the-world and on-the-earth. The world is open and revealing; the earth is self-closing and ever covering the deeper significance of earthly things. Among the ways that Heidegger defines an art work is that of the temple which "lets the god be present"[4] and thus art is a site where "man can be at home in his essence—in the world and on the earth" (Perotti, 83). Palés perceived this difference between world and earth as the surface mundane world and the numinous soul medium. Where he was able to bridge the world's possibilities and the deeper significance of the earth was in the poem. Thus Palés consistently designed his poems as passages from the mundane to an experience with the numinous. But Palés had long established this design as a stylistic hallmark, much before Heidegger would have been widely translated.

In the question of poetry, therefore, Heidegger at best would have reaffirmed a vision that Palés had already developed over the years. Heidegger also defined poetry as the naming of "what is holy"[5] because poetry is the "inaugural naming of Being and of the essence of all things."[6] And because poetry is the essence of all things, existence is a "fundamentally poetic"[7] experience that we begin to understand not through metaphysics but primitively, by Being-in-the-world as we reside on-the-earth, by "dwelling poetically," a phrase Heidegger cited from Hölderlin: "to 'dwell poetically' means: to stand in the presence of the gods and to be involved in the proximity of the essence of things." (Heidegger, 35). This essentially parallels Palés's notion of the poem as the point of contact between the mundane and the spiritual.

Revealing the essence of things, then, for both Palés and Heidegger, poetry is not made of language; rather "the essence of language must be understood through the essence of poetry" (Heidegger, 35), owing to whose presence language itself becomes the House of Being. In Palés's poetry, in this "House of Being" the essence of language is a woman—"Diosa-Poesía," "Filí-Melé," or "Tembandumba." These three numina, representative of three phases of Palés's work, are threaded by Palés's appreciation from the start of his career that "Poetry is the primitive language of a historical people" (Heidegger, 36), "history" here meaning living in time.

Through a work of art, of which Heidegger considered poetry the highest form, the World and the Earth make contact. The World provides the ideas, desires and lights while the Earth provides the raw materials, the stone or colors of the work. "The world absorbs those materials into its light, so that they yield up meaning. . . . But the earth does not give itself over completely. It forces the world to stick its tentacles into its resistance. . . . Thus the temple takes its meaning from its site and is rooted in it."[8] But this Heideggerian relationship between World and Earth is also extremely sexual and procreative. Thus it is not uncommon to find Heidegger or his interpreters resorting to the description of what the person receives by "dwelling poetically," i.e., intimately with the resistant Earth, with metaphors of a pregnant woman, a lover, a mother. Consistent with that imagery, in Palés's poetry the existential essence always has the form of a woman. Whether as Filí-Melé or in a "tú" image, she assumes the incarnations of a pregnant woman, a *virgo mater*, an embodiment of a perfect giving that is simultaneously a taking, a fleeing that is an arriving and the source of all love and all nurturing. Her love is synonymous with existence.

Unfortunately, while that philosophical side to Palés has been critically sidestepped, too much has been made of Palés's amorous life as the subject of the "Filí-Melé" cycle. The legend of Palés's unrequited love for a woman he called "Filí-Melé" has resulted in readers interpreting strictly as love poems to that woman the two poems in which Filí-Melé is the named love object. In her chronology in the Ayacucho edition, to illustrate, Arce de Vázquez makes a point of noting that in 1949 Palés was smitten with a woman he would call "Filí-Melé," a much younger *mulata*. Of course, for the aging, now Afro-Antillean-souled Palés, that impossible woman was also a symbol of his identity, which, as Arce also informs us, motivated him to produce (apparently by appending stanzas) "the second version of Mulata-Antilla" (Palés, 388). Arce also tells us that in that year Palés started writing "el ciclo de los poemas de Filí-Melé," although it is unclear whether she meant those two poems expressly about "Filí-Melé," or included the sonnets, not normally identified with her when one refers to "los poemas de Filí-Melé." However one prefers to read Palés's love history into these poems and the touch of realism by using the pet name "Filí-Melé" he gave that younger woman, in the poems themselves something more complex takes place. Owing to the span between their ages, the impossibility of having his love requited also aroused in Palés questions about existence and the essence of things, so that his passion eventually was as metaphysical as it was physical, and his impossible pursuit of an impossible love ultimately turned into a metaphor of an attempt to regain his vitality in poetry, which in his old age rejected him like "Filí-Melé."

Similarly, we must revise our approach to the two "Filí-Melé" poems and begin to see them as cyclic high points spun off from the cluster of sonnets that make up the complete "Filí-Melé" cycle:

["La Caza Inútil" ("The Futile Chase")]
"A Nimia Vicens" ("To Nimia Vicens")
"Boceto" ("Sketch")
"Mujer Encinta" ("Pregnant Woman")
"Virgo Mater"
"Para lo Eterno" ("For the Eternal/Stop the Eternal")
"Asteriscos para lo Intacto" ("Asterisks for the Intact")
["El Llamado" ("The Call/The Called One")]
"Puerta al Tiempo en Tres Voces" ("Entrance to Time in Three Voices")
"La Búsqueda Asesina" ("The Killer Search/The Search Kills")

All these poems share two stylistic elements:

1. They are all love poems to a love object that assumes different external manifestations—a mother, the essence of Nimia Vicens' poetry, the mythic "Virgo Mater," a "Boceto" of her fleetingness—but is always the same love object.

2. The extended discourse across a diversity of poems is expressed by a shared lexicon of recurring imagery such as *magia, luz, gracia, música, armonía, amor.*

In brackets above, the first listed poem "La Caza Inútil," didn't appear in the 1957 De Onís selection,[9] and was first published in Arce de Vázquez's edition among three previously unpublished poems, the last three in the book. Despite its being placed by Arce among the last poems, suggesting that this poem is chronologically one of Palés's last, the poem better serves here as an introduction and gloss on the cycle's central theme:

> Se acabó la palabra al borde mismo
> de contenerte en última vislumbre.
> Trampa de polvo azul sobre el abismo
> a ti, diafana pieza de la cumbre.
>
> [The word ended at the very brink
> of comprehending you in a final glimpse.
> A blue powder trap over the abyss
> to you, the summit's crystalline prize.]

As occurs in the range of Palés's poems, the setting is the imagination or "sueño" in which he is involved in a chase. The object of his pursuit is the "ineffable cipher of poetry," the essence of poetry. This confirmation is kept from the surface text of the cycle's other poems until "La Búsqueda Asesina." The loved, unnamed "tú" exists separate from the pursuer but his pursuit of her is fused to her flight:

> Día tras día renuncio de buscarte,
> pero vuelvo al quehacer más trascendido,
> y más iluminado de encontrarte.
>
> [Day after day I renounce looking for you,
> but return to the most transcendent,
> most luminous occupation of finding you.]

Thus his "Futile Chase" is finally defined as the "gracia del arte" that unites the poet and the poetic essence in an "órbita amorosa," the writing of his poetry, the site where he endeavors to find her. This poem, then, whether it preceded or followed the cycle proper aptly serves as a gloss on it.

What keeps it out of the sonnet grouping of the cycle is that it is self-contained; the sonnets form a sequence linked by the final stanza of one poem and the subsequent poem's opening lines and theme.[10] The perfume and movement images in the last line of "A Nimia Vicens," for example, are followed by "Boceto," about the love object's lightness and aerial movement. Similarly, the "don creador" in the final stanza of "Boceto" is followed by "Mujer Encinta," whose final image of regeneration is followed by "Virgo Mater," the last sonnet, which in turn ends with the word "eterna" and is thus followed by "Para lo Eterno," the first of the cycle's grouping of poems that are not sonnets.

"A Nimia Vicens" ("To Nimia Vicens") is a highly ambiguous poem, shifting between being about the poet Vicens and being about her poetry:

> Catedral de jazmín hecha en la brisa,
> llena el mundo de aroma tu nevar.
> ¡Oh casa de la espuma y la sonrisa
> para el sueño, la nube y el cantar!

> [Jasmine cathedral erected in the breeze,
> your snowing petals perfume the world.
> Oh house of the wave's foam and the smile,
> for the dream, the cloud, the song!]

The second stanza changes the subject to "El verbo," the words "imbued with your essence":

> El verbo, penetrado de tu esencia,
> embriágase en fulgor de amanecer;
> y en el leve fluir de tu presencia
> la gracia es don y la bondad quehacer.

> [The word, imbued with your essence,
> drinks dawn's radiance till drunk;
> and in your being's weightless flow
> grace is a talent, generosity a calling.]

The subsequent sestet repeats the jasmine metaphor, which had originally referred to Vicens, but now applies to "verbo." The following line plays with ambiguity:

> Luminero que el tiempo emprimavera . . .
> forma de esta poesía, tan ligera,
> que se deshoja al sólo dar su olor.

[Jasmine grove that time turns into spring . . .
form of this poetry, so light,
that just in giving us its scent its petals fall.]

The "forma" of the poetry is "tan ligera," which in describing
poetry is not necessarily praise. And to "deshojar" [lose its petals]
upon giving its fragrance is not entirely flattering. The verb *deshojar* also connotes to give a rhetorical display and, used in conjunction with the negative meaning of "ligera," further tinges Palés
praise of Vicens' poetry with a subtle criticism of its being too
thin. This critique accounts for the second tercet's opening with
"Pero":

Pero en el ritmo que su voz asume,
todo es ensueño y música y perfume
porque a su paso el mundo se hace flor.

[But in the rhythm that its voice assumes,
everything is dream and music and perfume
because as it passes the world turns into flower.]

Rich in "ritmo," if not so much in substance, her poetry invokes
a state of dream and perfume of the poetic essence. The rhythm
of her poetry's voice telescopes into the gait of the poetic essence,
not Vicens herself. Out of the numinous site of Vicens's poetry,
then, the true poetic essence enters the world, walks by and produces an ambiguity in the text: on the one hand, her fragrance
and fallen petals beautify the world into a "flor"; on the other
hand, Poetry's gait inebriates the world and on her passing elicits
from it a *flor* or compliment of her beauty.

"Boceto" expands on the movement image in the last line of
"A Nimia Vicens." Employing a *como*-simile to compare the *tú*-
essence with "aire detenido," the poem reiterates the impossibility of arriving at anything but an ethereal "Boceto" ("Sketch") of
this woman-essence. A mass of "suspended air," she is also a
"flight," ever drawn to a numinous "floating country."

Eres como de aire detenido
en lámina de música ondulante,
te mueves, vuelo hacia país flotante,
por alígero numen concebido.

[You are as if of an air suspended
on a sheet of undulating music,

you move, flight toward a floating country,
by a winged, imagined numen.]

Her step/flight produces an arcing light that converts her into an "eje luminoso" ("luminous axis") and a giver of light, light meaning poetry in the lexicon. Her poetry-emitting walk in the subsequent sestet is of music or "armonía," also poetry in the lexicon:

A cada movimiento del movido
volar de tu pisar, arco radiante
trémulo irradia de tu pie volante
en eje luminoso convertido.

Una, dos, tres pisadas armoniosas,
cuatro, cinco, seis ruedas luminosas
con tu planta por mágico sustento.

[With each movement of your step's
rapid flight, a radiant arc
scintillates from each flying foot,
suddenly a luminous axis.

One, two, three harmonious steps,
four, five, six, luminous wheels,
as magic levitates your soles.]

The composite image is of a gait/rhythm that emits light/poetry, just like the gait/rhythm of the "Diosa-Poesía" in "Las Torres Blancas." The "Sketch," the poet realizes, is of the genius of creativity, "light and movement":

Pienso, al mirar lo que tu ser despide,
que en la cadencia de tu andar reside
el don creador de luz y movimiento.

[I believe, after watching what your being emits
that in the cadence of your walk resides
the creator gift of light and movement.]

This "don creador," which also plays with the idea of *señor creador*, or God, is the subject of the sonnet "Mujer Encinta." Dedicated to the presumably pregnant "Marilú de Rodríguez," the poem celebrates pregnant womankind as a site of numinous creativity. In her stare, a "languid bleating" dreams. This sound image telescopes into the visual image of that sound as a "a

humid-moss vegetable voice / that rises out of the beloved soul."
Abstracted into a geometric form, her lying body forms a curved
horizontal line separating her exterior from her interior being.
That interiority becomes the depth in which "the red harp of
beats" creates music strummed by a hand of "air-light-blood," a
fusion of images where, according to the lexicon, "light" signifies
poetry, existence or enlightment, "air" signifies the hand's metaphysical properties, and "blood" the physical properties:

> Horizonte de curva renovada
> al contorno del cuerpo devenido,
> y al fondo, la arpa roja del latido,
> por mano de aire luz sangre pulsada.
>
> [Horizon of a curvature remodeled
> to fit the swollen body's contour,
> and deep down, the red harp of beats
> plucked by a hand of air-light-blood.]

The poem's metaphysical theme is elaborated in the following
two tercets. On the surface of that "Curving horizon" is the slow
heavy movement of creation, "existence anchored," while inside
reigns the dynamism of numinous activity. God, a lover of harmony, music in the lexicon, is the one who plays "the red harp."
   The next poem, "Virgo Mater," translates the "Mujer Encinta"
into the virgin motherhood myth and metaphorically link's God's
biological creation to the numinous creativity of the as yet unnamed Filí-Melé's perpetual state of maternity:

> Fuerte como la espuma que siempre se rehace,
> tu alma, todos los días, de su misterio nace,
> y vive eternamente virgen, reciénnacida, . . .
>
> [Strong as sea foam in endless self-rebirth,
> daily your soul springs from its mystery
> and lives eternally virgin, eternally just born.]

Note the pun: "re-cien (veces) nacida" and "recién nacida".
   Affected by neither time nor space, the *virgo mater*'s soul is
compared to God who, as in "Mujer Encinta," extracts worlds "de
la nada." Eternal as God, the virgin mother's soul is indestructible
and, on being destroyed "apenas," a pun suggesting "a penas,"
she regenerates:

> Nada conturba su ámbito: ni el tiempo detenido,
> ni el ilusorio juego del espacio fluido . . .

es como Dios forjando sus mundos de la nada,
apenas se destruye cuando ya está creada.

[Nothing ripples its surface: neither time stopped,
nor the illusory game of flowing space . . .
it's like God forging his hands from nothing:
hardly destroyed, it's already created.]

"Creada" also opens the first tercet and begins an extended image of the "tú" or "Virgo Mater" as a perpetually renewed wave of the "mar sin orilla del amor" ["love's shoreless sea"], water being one of Palés's recurring numinous images:

Creada ya y formándose de nuevo, ola constante
que un hálito de vida mantiene renovada
en avatar perenne y en gracia palpitante,

y tan fiel al principio de su esencia materna,
que en el mar sin orillas del amor proyectada
tu alma es vieja y es joven y es fugaz y es eterna.

[Already created and forming anew, constant wave
that a breath of life keeps ever renewed
in perpetual avatar and vibrating grace,

and so true to the source of its maternal essence
that cast upon the shoreless sea of love
your soul is old and young and fleeting and forever.]

The final "eterna" connects "Virgo Mater" to the cycle's next poem, "Para lo Eterno" ("For the Eternal/Stop the Eternal") a title in which "para" punningly works as both preposition and verb, epitomizing the poem's dual objectives: to address and also freeze the eternal. In this poem, we immediately note that the prominently positioned copulative verb is in the imperfective subjunctive mood. Whereas in the indicative of the previous poems we saw only her image (the predicate nominative), by expressing the hypothetical, the subjunctive heightens our sense of her being even more ethereal than the previous ethereal images:

Fueras céfiro, brisa, criatura
de ingravidez, de gracia transparente.
Crecieras suave, música emoliente . . .

[Were you zephyr, breeze, creature
without gravity, of transparent grace.
Grown smoothly, an emollient music . . .]

Besides the subjunctive mood device, the stanza also employs images that either appear in another cyclic poem or throughout Palés's work: the "brisa" is found in "A Nimia Vicens," "gracia" is present throughout the cycle, as well as the Palesian image of woman as a spreading presence ("Crecieras suave, música emoliente").

The second and third stanzas, reiterating the simultaneous movement and non-movement in "Boceto" and other sonnets in the cycle, describe the speaker's dream of her as a spreading ethereal essence yet frozen in time and space, emitting a scent of jasmine, speaking with the numinous "harp's voice," and luminated internally with her "own voice":

> O inmóvil en tu pálida belleza
> quedáraste en un limbo, ensimismada:
> ojos serenos, mano reposada,
> y jugando a ser triste sin tristeza.
>
> Al tiempo y al espacio congelada,
> lucieras en tu lánguido hemisferio
> marea de jazmín, voz de salterio,
> y por tu propia luz iluminada.
>
> [Oh sculpted in your pale beauty,
> would you stayed in a limbo, abstracted:
> calm eyes, lax hand,
> and without sadness playing sad.
>
> Frozen in time and space,
> would you shone in your languid hemisphere
> a jasmine tide, a flute's voice,
> and aglow with your own inner light.]

The fourth stanza employs the motives of the spreading woman-essence and the eternal waves. It also evokes the self-generating maternal image of the soul in "Virgo Mater" and the numinous activity of the womb in "Mujer Encinta":

> Ampliárase tu luz por la vacía
> perennidad en ola sin ruido,
> sangre empujada al diáfano latido
> de una interior, angélica armonía.
>
> [Would your light radiate across
> the empty continuity in a roarless wave,
> blood pumped to the diaphanous beat
> of an inner, angelic harmony.]

The "propia luz" in the third stanza, then, is actually (on the semantic level) telescoped from and (on the surface level) telescopes to the "blood pumped to the diaphanous beat / of an inner, angelic harmony." These lines parallel those of "Mujer Encinta" where inside her the beating heart is portrayed as a red harp being played by the hand of God, a music lover "gozoso de armonía."

But in "Para lo Eterno," the discourse remains hypothetical, dreamed by a speaker who expresses no hope of realizing his dream. Hence the main clause, the final stanza, is also in the imperfective subjunctive, evoking an imperfective sense of his fantasy:

> Así te amara en trance reverente,
> inefable sentir mi sentir fuera
> y fijáraste en gracia y en manera
> de ser para lo eterno, eternamente.

> [So would I love you in reverential trance,
> unspeakable feeling my feeling would be
> and you would freeze in your grace and in your manner
> of belonging to the eternal eternally.]

The perfect, indestructible circularity of the woman-essence is the subject of "Asteriscos para lo Intacto," whose title also hints at ungrammatically punning with "para" and thus reinforcing the contradiction of the title: asterisks added to the intact obviously "paran" or interrupt that quality of being "intacto." Formally, this poem has the distinguishing feature of comprising rhythmic couplets, each of whose lines evokes a hemisphere that together evoke a sense of complement and wholeness:

> Por repartida que vayas
> entera siempre estarás.
> Aún dándote de mil modos
> no te fragmentas jamás.

> [No matter how parceled
> ever whole you'll be.
> Doled a thousand ways,
> fragments you'll never be.]

The first line hinges on the ambiguity of "repartida," understood as either its common semantic meaning, "apportioned," or its literal meaning, "fragmented." Either way, the "tú" breaks up to remain whole, a wholeness that the rhyme and couplet arrangement both reinforce. By repeating this rhythmic pattern (unique among the cyclic poems) "Asteriscos" also evokes a sense of the eternal "oleaje" imaged in "Para lo Eterno," a use of rhythm reminiscent of *Tuntún de Pasa y Grifería*. On the semantic level, these rhythmic waves foreground the contradiction of the essence's being whole and ever giving of herself, her metaphysical impossibility:

> Cada donación que haces,
> cada dádiva que das,
> te deja siempre en lo mismo
> a repartir o donar . . .
> prodigio del dar y ser,
> milagro del ir y estar.

> [Every donation you make,
> each gift you extend,
> leaves you ever unchanged
> to dispense or donate . . .
> prodigy of giving and being,
> miracle of going and staying.]

The poem then compares the "*tú*" to those images— light, love, eternity, all familiar from the lexicon—that share her metaphysical capability:

> Darte es tenerte a ti misma
> y tenerte es darte más;
> darse y tenerse ¿no es eso
> amor, luz, eternidad?
> El amor se da y se tiene,
> la luz se tiene y de da,
> y lo eterno vase dando
> y teniéndose eternal.

> [Giving you is having yourself
> and having yourself is giving of you more;
> having and giving, isn't that
> love, light, eternity?
> Love is to give and have,
> light is to have and give,
> and the eternal proceeds giving itself
> and having itself eternally.]

The poem continues as a conceit of metaphysical contradictions, evoking an obliteration of our rational sense of time and space. But by this time we must remind ourselves who the *tú* is, which we recall from the title is "lo Intacto," and we must also ask ourselves what is Palés's point. To be understood, "Para lo Eterno" and "Asteriscos para lo Intacto" must be read in the context of the cycle. The sonnets served as detailed studies of the *tú*, highlighting eternally poetic or creative or procreative powers. These first two nonsonnets, then, describe her movements, her irrational nature, and also serve as segues to the cycle's major poems.

The first of these is "El Llamado," which is in brackets in the list at the start of this chapter because, although thematically related, it differs in several ways from the poems that obviously belong to the cycle. To begin with, it lacks a *tú* as an image of the woman-essence. Here she is present as "ella." (In this poem, the *tú* is Death.) What justifies our reading of this poem as part of the cycle is that, like the *tú* or Filí-Melé, "ella" is the poet's life-force, a metaphysical contradiction, and her form is also a spreading, ethereal, inebriating presence:

> Miro esa dulce fábrica rendida,
> cuerpo de trampa y presa
> cuyo ritmo esencial como jugando
> manufactura la caricia aérea,
> el arrullo narcótico y el beso
> —víspera ardiente de gozosa queja—
> y me digo: Ya todo ha terminado . . .
>
> [I see that soft, enthralled factory,
> body both a trap and a prize,
> whose essential rhythm like playing
> manufactures the aerial caress,
> the narcotic lulling and the kiss
> —ardent eve of a pleasurable plaint—
> and I tell myself: Everything is finished . . .

Being in love with "ella" produces the same thing that transpired when he wrote his poems, his being transported to a numinous place. Consequently, when she opens her eyes the poet embarks on his passage to a numinous remote shore from where "algo" in the depths of her eyes invites and transports him.

Poetry (the pleasure of writing it), then, is "el amor" with which he wishes to remain on earth. This "amor," which had transported him to numinous shores, had been his connection between the spiritual realm and the world. He could travel to or invoke the numen but always return. But when the messenger of death comes, the poet must leave his "amor" for a permanent, remote, numinous place he calls "allá":

> Emisario solicíto que vienes
> con oculto mensaje hasta mi puerta,
> sé lo que te propones
> y no me engaña tu misión secreta;
> me llaman desde allá,
> pero el amor dormido aquí en la hierba
> es bello todavía
> y un júbilo de sol baña la tierra.
> ¡Déjame tu implacable poderío
> una hora, un minuto más con ella!
>
> [Solicitous emissary who arrives
> with a hidden message at my door,
> I am privy to your purpose
> and not fooled by your secret mission;
> they're calling me from out there,
> but the love asleep here on the grass
> is beautiful still
> and a sunlight joy bathes the land.
> Allow me your inexorable power
> one hour, one more minute with her!

The final two lines are syntactically ambiguous: sounding on the one hand as if the poet were addressing the messenger, "implacable poderío." But the commas are missing, so the "implacable poderío" becomes what the poet wants to enjoy with her, whether for an hour, or just a minute. In sum, in "El Llamado" is the first sign of Palés's reflecting on what he would miss about his life's coming to an end: being a poet, the lover of "ella."

All the stylistic and semantic elements of the previously discussed poems converge in the two poems explicitly about "Filí-Melé," "Puerta al Tiempo en Tres Voces" and "La Búsqueda Asesina." These two poems expand on the fear in "El Llamado," reflecting philosophically on the meaning of poetry. Also, Palés's obsession with the metaphysically elusive quality of the poetic essence reveals itself to be part of a broader obsession with a life-force and creative potency that threaten to leave him. Palés's having fallen in love with an exceptionally beautiful young dark woman provided him with a perfect metaphor for the "Futile

Chase." The former "tú" and "Ella" then emerge as "Filí-Melé," the name he gave his uncooperative love object.

Of the two poems specifically about her, "Puerta al Tiempo en Tres Voces" appears to come first, enjoying the revived vitality of Palés's attempting to evoke in verbal images the metaphysical concept that lay underneath all his visions of a numinous realm beyond the mundane. In the first section of that poem, Filí-Melé is first compared to a tree, a metaphor that is telescoped from the "aire detenido" in "Boceto." And like the water-quartz image in "Asteriscos," that tree is also crystalline, transparent:

> I
> . . . Del trasfondo de un sueño la escapada
> Filí-Melé. La fluida cabellera
> fronda crece, de abejas enjambrada;
> el tronco—desnudez cristalizada—
> es desnudez en luz tan desnudada . . .
> que al mirarlo se mira la mirada.

> [. . . From the background of a dream the escaped
> Filí-Melé. Her streaming hair,
> sprouts fronds, is hived by bees;
> her trunk—a nudity crystallized—
> is bareness in a light so bare
> that your gaze upon it gazes on your gaze.]

The tree metaphor also parallels the one in "Canción de la Vida Media" in which, as now, the poems are depicted as *frutos*. The tree in "Puerta," however, adds the detail of the "vena," which sustains the sense of a living organism and, on another level, employs the figurative meaning of vein as poetic inspiration. Like a human vein, the tree's is also blue, the color that symbolizes poetry, a residual *modernista* convention. Through that vein, Filí-Melé's colorless"pálida tinta" dissolves to flow into the current of existence, which inexorably flows toward death:

> Frutos hay, y la vena despertada
> látele azul y en el azul diluye
> su pálida tintura derramada,
> por donde todo hacia la muerte fluye
> en huida tan luene y sosegada
> que nada en ella en apariencia huye.

> ¡Fruits hang, and the aroused vein
> beats blue and in the blue dissolves

her pale tincture shed
into the tide everything rides toward death,
in a flight so dreamed and peaceful
that no detail of her appears to flee.]

But Filí-Melé's dissolving in that current does not mean she dies. Being a numen and a Palesian woman image, Filí-Melé spreads out into eternity, in a flight described without a specific verb of movement, evoked by the rhythm of the lines:

Filí-Melé Filí-Melé, ¿hacia dónde
tú, si no hay tiempo para recogerte
ni espacio donde puedas contenerte?

[Filí-Melé Filí-Melé, toward where
you, if no time lasts to gather you,
no space holds your dimensions?]

Being beyond time and space, yet captured by the poem, she is both "inaprehensible" and "atrapada." And being the numinous essence of Being and poetry, she is the essence of non-Being. Hence she is also "esencia de la muerte":

Filí, la inaprehensible ya atrapada,
Melé, numen y esencia de la muerte.

[Filí, the uncatchable now trapped,
Melé, numen and essence of death.]

The first section ends with Filí-Melé going off "ahora," an image that refers to her existence at the moment the poem is being written or read. He answers his own question with a second question: her white sails sail off to the remote shores of the numinous watery realm that reappears in Palés's poems. She is returning to the "allá" from where the poet is called in "El Llamado," to Tembandumba's Quimbamba:

¿Para qué ribera
huye tu blanca vela distendida
sobre mares oleados de quimera?

[Toward what shore
flies your white stretched sail
over swelling, chimera-slicked seas?]

In the second part, the poet attempts to poetically capture the numinous site (of his "caza inútil") where she dwells fleetingly:

II

En sombra de sentido de palabras,
fantasmas de palabras;
en el susto que toma a la palabras
cuando con leve, súbita pisada,
las roza el halo del fulgor del alma;
—rasgo de ala en el agua,
ritmo intentado que no logra acorde,
abortada emoción cohibida de habla—;
en el silencio tan cercano al grito
que recorre las noches estrelladas,
y más lo vemos que lo oímos,
y casi le palpamos la sustancia;
o en el silencio plano y amarillo
de las desiertas playas,
batiendo el mar en su tambor de arena
salado puño de ola y alga.

[In shadows of meanings of words,
phantoms of words;
in the fright that overtakes words
when with weightless, unexpected footsteps,
against them brushes the brilliance of the soul's halo
—fin's stroke in the water,
effort at rhythm that fails to harmonize,
aborted, muzzled emotion—
in the silence so close to being a scream
it travels across starry nights
and more than hear we see it,
and almost touch its substance;
or over the flat, yellow silence
of deserted beaches.
the sea pounding on its drum of sand
a briny, wave-and-algae fist]

This catalog of phrases and clauses ultimately has no main clause, and its dominant image is the syntax itself. Following the syntactic pattern throughout Palés's work, they are all foregrounded adverbials that call attention to Filí-Melé's elusive site and presence. At this point, having defined her evoked her in words, Palés inquires whether his style will serve to invoke her:

¿Qué lenguaje te encuentra, con qué idioma
(ojo inmóvil, voz muda, mano laxa)

podré yo asirte, columbrar tu imagen,
la imagen de tu imagen reflejada
más allá de la música-poesía,
muy atrás de los cantos sin palabras?

What idiom finds you, with what language
(glued eye, mute voice, relaxed hand)
capture you, make out your image,
the image of your image mirrored
far beyond music-poetry,
long before songs without words?

Both "cantos sin palabras," meaning poetry and music and
"música-poesía," meaning song, invoke the numen. Both genres
use words, casting a "sombra de sentido" ["shade of meaning"]
in which she dwells. The words contain the poet's desires that
stretch out thin to reach her:

Mis palabras, mis sombras de palabras,
a ti, en la punta de sus pies, aupadas.
Mis deseos, mis galgos de deseos;
a ti, ahilados, translúcidos espectros.

[My words, my shadows of words,
propped up on tippy toes for you.
My desires, my grayhound desires,
translucent ghosts stretched thin toward you.]

His words, like children, are held up on their toes to reach Filí-
Melé. His desires, like bony greyhounds emaciated from old age
and from years of pursuing, also look to her. This is all he is
capable of in his expression of desire. He is the pathetic open net
over the bottomless abyss (a parallel to the "blue powder trap
over the abyss" in "The Futile Chase"); she is ever absent and
unattainable:

Yo, evaporado, diluido, roto,
abierta red en el sinfín sin fondo . . .
Tú, por ninguna parte de la nada,
¡qué escondida, cuán alta!

[I, evaporated, diluted, broken,
open net in bottomless infinity . . .
You, nowhere in nothingness,
how ensconced, how high!]

The word "alta" points to the inevitable numinous destination, which in Palés's poems, even though the passage may begin downward or across, is ultimately celestial.

The third part informs us that rational intellection destroys our vision of the essence. She exists in the flash of creativity, in the instant we dream, like the impossible images "catedral de ceniza, arbol de niebla," which we can only envision fleetingly in a poetic evocation:

> III
>
> En lo fugaz, en lo que ya no existe
> cuando se piensa,
> y apenas deja de pensarse
> cobra existencia;
> en lo que si se nombra se destruye,
> catedral de ceniza, arbol de niebla . . .
> ¿Cómo subir tu rama?
> ¿Cómo tocar tu puerta?
>
> [In the fleeting, in what no longer exists
> once it is thought,
> and in a blink after not thinking it
> regains existence;
> in that which if named is destroyed,
> a cathedral of ash, a tree of mist . . .
> How to climb your branch?
> How to pound your door?]

The "cathedral of ash" and "tree of mist," once frozen in words lose their lightness, their possibility as they existed in the imagination before the words froze them. That lost essence of poetry is the elusive thing of beauty that the words cannot match. So too, being able to make an image of Filí-Melé is not to possess that inspiriting essence for which he longs.

The answer to the poet's dilemma is the same given in "La Caza Inútil": that in the chase he has her purity; the writing of the poem captures her essence. Between the two lovers, the poet extends "un puente de armonioso llanto," meaning poetry (interpreting "armonioso" according to the cycle's lexicon), that creation of words that takes us beyond them, to the song without words, a fragile bridge built of the poet's desires that were already said to be weak and emaciated as a "grayhound." Thus only the poem's significant silence, described earlier as "so close to a scream" can cross over:

Pienso que de tu pena hasta la mía
se tiende un puente de armonioso llanto
tan quebradizo y frágil, que en la sombra
sólo puede el silencio atravesarlo.

[I believe that from your sorrow to mine
spans a bridge of harmonious weeping,
so brittle and fragile, that in shadow
only silence can walk across it.]

This bridge of words-now-poem—and therefore no longer
words—is held up by "estribos de aire amargo," abutments of air
hardened by life's bitterness. Should the bridge's "estribos" fail,
any semantically significant facial gesture or "mirada" would be
enough to reach her on the other side:

Un gesto, una mirada, bastarían
a fallar sus estribos de aire amargo.

[One gesture, one look, would suffice,
collapsed its abutments of bitter air.]

But here (impossible to render in translation), "estribos" functions ambiguously, also referring to Filí-Melé's ears' "stirrup
bones of bitter air" across which words convey their meanings.
Should these collapse the poet would also have to rely on gestures
and looks.

Palés then compares this semantically significant "gesto" and
"mirada" to the music of Carl María Fredrich von Weber (1786–
1826) who in 1823 composed *Euryanthe*, an opera unique in the
history of music owing to its consisting solely of music, gestures
and looks. *Euryanthe* was in fact not Weber's "último canto," although it was in the sense of his being his most ingenious achieve-
ment. Palés's swan song metaphor is based on Weber's having
written *Oberan* in the year of his death. Confusing the dates of the
two operas, Palés apparently believed that *Euryanthe* was Weber's
swan song "sin palabras.") Should the poet's poetry-bridge to the
numinous essence collapse (and he thus fail to attain her), the
significant silence of gestures and looks would become his
swan song:

Canto final donde la acción frustrada
abre al tiempo una puerta sostenida
en tres voces que esperan tu llegada; . . .

> tu llegada, aunque sé que eres perdida . . .
> Perdida y ya por siempre conquistada,
> fiel fugada Filí-Melé abolida.
>
> [Final song in which the frustrated act
> opens to time an entrance in sharps
> in three voices that await your arrival; . . .
> your arrival, though I know you are lost . . .
> Lost and now forever conquered,
> faithful, fleeting, abolished Filí-Melé.]

The "puerta sostenida" is a musical entrance in sharp notes ("sostenida") coming from three muse-like voices that await the arrival of Filí-Melé. But what three voices? The musical voices of present, past and future, as we experience them in language; Filí-Melé exists in all three tenses simultaneously. The three voices may also be grammatical *voces*, the active and passive and the one Palés attempts to create in the poem, an active (pursuit)/passive (resignation). These *voces* also capture her arrival in imagery, as any instant of her being is at once past, already future and permanently frozen in the present/past/future in the poem:

> tu llegada, aunque sé que (ya) eres perdida . . .
> (ya) perdida y (ya) por siempre conquistada,
> fiel (ya) fugada Filí-Melé abolida.

The seemingly contradictory past participle modifiers *(perdida, conquistada, fugada, abolida)* harmonize because Filí-Melé's existence is distinct from her imagistic presence. Like "lo intacto" and "lo eterno" of the earlier poems in the cycle, she defies logic by giving of herself and remaining complete; she can escape from the poet and continue to dwell in the poem. Hence she is lost forever and is destined to ever be "conquistada" by the poet. Curiously, an older meaning of the word is "to pursue intensely." So the word encapsules that she will continue to be "conquistada," pursued intensely and thus in pursuit "possessed."

"La Búsqueda Asesina (Poema Inconcluso)," one of Palés's most intriguing poems, completes the cycle. What makes this poem unique is the manner in which it structurally responds to the discourse, allowing itself to die when Filí-Melé is declared dead, and changing rhythm, tone, and focus, as if the poem survives when Filí-Melé is again alive in memory. But these elements are best discussed at the moment that they appear in the poem, which opens with a lament over the feeling of loss of the desire to pursue and the awareness of having exhausted both the pursued and exhausted one's own life in the pursuit. The title therefore is intentionally ambiguous. The pursuit kills both the pursuer and the pursued, "The Killer Pursuit/The Pursuit Kills":

> Yo te maté, Filí-Melé: tan leve
> tu esencia, tan aérea tu pisada,
> que apenas ibas nube ya eras nieve,
> apenas ibas nieve ya eras nada.

> [I killed you, Filí-Melé: so bouyant
> your essence, so aerial your tread,
> who, one second a cloud, now was snow,
> only just snow, now was nothing.]

The ethereal images of constant changes are by now identifiable from the other poems in the cycle. The "milagro del ir y ser" and "prodigio del dar y ser" in "Asteriscos para lo Intacto" here becomes an "ir" and "ser" as Palés employs the "apenas ibas" to situate her fleeting in time before making her instantaneous change with the "ya eras." (Note the morphological ambiguity of "apenas," which homonymically also says "a penas," at the cost of sorrows.) This amorphous movement imagery is developed in the second stanza:

> Cambio de forma en tránsito constante,
> habida y transfugada a sueño, a bruma . . .
> Agua-luz lagrimándose en diamante,
> diamante sollozándose en espuma.

> [Change of form in constant passage,
> captured and defected to dream, to mist . . .
> Water-light teardrops accruing into diamond,
> diamond sobbing itself into foam.]

Being a metaphysical impossibility, she is compared to a music whose form and movement one cannot follow:

> Fugacidad, eternidad . . . ¿quién sabe?
> ¿Cómo seguir tu alado movimiento?
> ¿De qué sustancia figurar tu clave,
> y con qué clave descifrar tu acento?

> [Fleetingness, eternity . . . Who knows?
> How to follow your winged movement?

From what substance figure your key,
and with what key decode your accent?]

That same "movimiento" ambiguously alludes to the rhythm of the poem/song. The third line refers to the lack of a morphological substance that would give her form, and his inability to write down her musical key. Without her "clave," the poet cannot translate her musical "acento," which in poetry is rhythm and stress.

In the fourth stanza, the passage structure rises to the surface text to become part of the discourse. The poet feels that in pursuing her for so long he caused her death. On the other hand, he affirms that his pursuit of her was what led him to the numinous images of the shore and the water:

> Yo te maté, Filí-Melé; buscada
> a sordos tumbos ciegos, perseguida
> con voz sin cauce, con afán sin brida;
> allá en agua de sombras . . .

> [I killed you, Filí-Melé; sought
> with deaf blind stumblings, pursued
> with unchanneled voice, with unreined intensity;
> way out over shadowy water . . .]

The last line above introduces an extended description of Filí-Melé, with past participles modifiers placed at the end of each line. Their rhyming, like crashing waves, emphatically reminds us of her presence:

> allá en agua de sombras resbalada
> sobre arena de estrellas encendida;
> allá en tumulto de olas espumada
> —flor instantánea al aire suspendida—
> por la gracia y la luz arrebatada
> en aire sin recuerdo devenida.

> [far off on shadowy water flown
> on star-glistening sand inflamed;
> far off in waves' tumult frothed
> —instant flower in air suspended—
> by grace and light seized
> into an amnesiac air transformed.]

The flower image parallels the simile in "Boceto," in which the tú is compared to "stopped air." Also from the lexicon, once again the image of grace and light, poetry, which seized her and was the eventual cause of his extinguishing her. This daily deadly process is the thrust of the stanza's final lines, which returns to the poet's confession of how indefatigably he pursued her:

> De sol a sol, jornada tras jornada,
> desde la puesta hasta la amanecida;
> era viento de sangre para ahogarte,
> red de oscura pasión para envolverte.

> [Sun to sun, setting to rise,
> a day's measure to the next,
> I was a blood wind to drown you,
> a dark-passion net to engulf you.]

In the next two quatrains "luz" understood as poetry becomes part of the image "pan de luz," which combines images of his physical and spiritual elements of sustenance. Her aerial quality became a star, thus light-emitting, and in destroying her, "siderado / copo de espuma virgen," he not only extinguished her luminosity ("tu fulgor primero"), but he also began to kill himself, as she was pivotal to him in his spiritual interiority as well as in his mundane person. Inside him, she was his "presencia / vital de amor," and outside, in her absence from him, she was his existential essence and reason for living, i.e., the motivation for his life-giving (and now killing) pursuit. Together, as a spiritual and mundane element, what she was for him can be summed up in "poesía":

> ¡Oh lirio, oh pan de luz, oh siderado
> copo de espuma virgen que con fiero
> y súbito ademán hube tronchado!
> ¿Cómo volverte a tu fulgor primero?

> Eras en mí, dentro de mí, presencia
> vital de amor que el alma sostenía,
> y para mí, fuera de mí, en ausencia,
> razón del ser y el existir: poesía.

> [Oh lily, oh luminous bread, oh star-
> twinkling bower of virgin sea foam
> that my savage, sudden gesture cut down.
> How to bring back your first brilliance!

> You were in me, inside me, vital presence
> of a love that fed my soul;

and for me, outside me, in absence,
reason for being and existing: poetry.]

This stanza, with "poesía" as its final word ends the first *movement*, so to speak, of the poem, which does not have numbered sections. At this point the poet experiences a loss of direction as the poem temporarily fades into ellipses:

Y ahora,
silencio, soledad, quietud que añora . . .

[And now,
silence, solitude, a quietude that longingly remembers . . .]

The poem then undergoes a change of intensity and tone, a change consistent with its discourse. Deprived of her, instead of existing in the whirlwind of Being, he finds himself in the eye of Nothingness, which is metaphorically compared to the calm in the eye of a hurricane. Concomitantly, the poem itself has had to recover the energy it had lost by announcing Filí-Melé's demise. Thus the rhythm changes to one that evokes the rushing, circular hurricane winds of nothingness. Trapped in its center, without air, feelings, words or ideas, he finds himself in a nostalgic calm that remembers her, a remembrance that appears to suffice to give new energy to resuscitate both him and the poem so that he may lyrically lament:

¿Qué trompa de huracán hace más ruido
que este calmazo atroz que me rodea
y me tiene sin aire y sin sentido,
sordo de verbo y lóbrego de idea,
y que se anuda a mí con cerco fiero
en yelo ardiente y negro congelado,
cual detrito de acoso y desespero
por íntima tensión centrifugado?

[What hurricane trumpet blows louder
than this atrocious, encircling calm
that holds me without air or feelings,
deaf to words, my thoughts a fog,
and girds me with a merciless circle
of burning ice and frozen black,
like a debris of hounding and despair
orbited around me by an intimate force.]

Note the unusual or misspelled "yelo," which appears to be a form of the original Latin for ice, *gelu*, and which also plays with the Spanish spelling of an *anglicismo*, "yellow.")

Now that Filí-Melé is gone, the poet calls out to her, an act that also, by his longing for her, once again commences the pursuit. After all, spirits, gods, and numina, do not really die. Thus the poem is reborn and its tone and rhythm change once more. In the final stanza, the hurricane of Nothingness having been telescoped into an image of his centrigual relationship with Filí-Melé, he sees himself as a top, and she the cord that spins him. Only in that relationship is his life revitalized over and over again:

> Zumbel tú, yo peonza. Vuelva al tiro,
> aquel leve tirar sobre el quebranto
> que a masa inerte dábale pie y giro
> haciéndola cantar en risa y llanto
> y en sonrisa y suspiro . . .

> [You the cord, I the top. Spin it again,
> that light throw over the wreck
> that gave an inert mass a foot and path
> making it sing in laughter and tears
> and in smiles and sighs . . .]

Because in Spanish a top is colloquially said to *bailar* or dance, the metaphor of the spinning top reiterates the numen-invoking dances in the Afro-Antillean poems. Also, as was implicit in Palés's equating his poems with a drumbeat in *Tuntún*, this "dancing" of the poet is a metaphor of another numen-invoking activity: the writing of poetry. When the poetic essence throws the poem and it dances, it has a "pie," which ambiguously means both foot and basis for doing something, and a "giro," which signifies "spin/circulatation/dance/route," as well as a particular way of structuring his writing, a style. Dependent on her for his being, activated to "dance," he urges her to spin the top again:

> ¡Vuelva, zumbel, el tiro,
> que mientras tires tú me dura el canto!

> [Again, cord, the spin,
> for while you make me spin I sing my song.]

The spinning/dancing of the top becomes synonymous with the his song, the "canto," making the spinning/dancing a form of song without words.

But "canto," we must also recall, provided an opportunity for punning in "Pueblo Negro," and here the incorrigible punster Palés again uses the ambiguity one should by now come to expect of him. In addition to using the obvious meaning of "tirar" ("throw") and "canto" ("song"), Palés allows the coexistence of the informal senses of those two words: "canto," with its sexual connotation of female genitalia; "tirar" as sexual nuance of copulation. The result is an antipoem imbedded in what appears to be a tragic, existential love poem, transforming it and giving the poet and poem a rebirth. For Palés, ultimately sexuality and poetry were synonymous, creative forces—a conviction originally expressed in the celebration of sexual energy in the Afro-Antillean poems. This is why he identified all creativity with womankind, whose *canto*—in all senses of that word—was absolutely essential for him to continue as a poet, so he could continue his dance. The threat of losing his sexual drive, of losing Filí-Melé, and his capacity to make the poetic "canto" last would then be synonymous losses.

Postscript: The Poem as Altar and Liturgy

The Filí-Melé cycle confirms that nearing the end of his life Palés finally became conscious that every poem was an altar, a site on which to invoke the numinous elements, what Heidegger called the "permanent." Composed of words, the poem is also a liturgy, or a groping toward a grammar of that liturgy by which the poem is turned into a numinous site. Everything depends on the correct words that will invite the essence of Being to the poem so that the poet may regenerate his sense of existence: "What idiom will find you, with what language/ . . . /capture you, ..." In attaching this metaphysical function to poetry both Palés and Heidegger again coincide. For in "Puerta," the dominant image is "la palabra," through which Palés aspires to evoke the "numen," which Heidegger called the "permanent":

> Poetry is the act of establishing by the word and in the word. What is established in this manner? The permanent. But can the permanent be established then? Is it not that which has always been present? No. Even the permanent must be fixed so that it will not be carried away, the simple must be wrested from confusion, proportion must be set before what lacks proportion. That which supports Being must be opened out, so that the existent may appear. But this very permanent is the transitory. (Heidegger, 34)

Like Heidegger, then, Luis Palés Matos was attracted to an authenticity perceived as deeper than the material self and not accessible through rational investigation. Thus, to experience the word in another, irrational way, Palés turned his poems into drumbeats *(tuntunes)*. That is why throughout his work and not exclusively in the Afro-Antillean poetry the quality of sounds, as well as ambiguities of all sorts (syntactic, morphological, semantic) are allowed to arouse other levels of reading, so that in "the shade of meanings of words," one experiences what he eventually called the "numen," the essence of the experience underlying the sound-words. Also, like Heidegger, Palés's return to the primitive was completely contradictory to his artistic and cultural style: Heidegger attempted to deconstruct the philosophical tradition

184

in which he worked and Palés the sophisticate, the Gongorine, who understood the unruliness of words and forged his poetry like a craftsman in metals, simultaneously intended an immaterial, primitive otherness to seep through the medium of his highly ritualized composition.

But if this complex imagination has been lost in the superficial *readings* of his Afro-Antillean poetry (the poems themselves being far more sophisticated even on an ethnologically thematic or imagistic level than heretofore has been appreciated), the Filí-Melé cycle reaffirms that Luis Palés Matos's poems throughout his career were intended as sophisticated instruments of thought as well as artifacts of beauty. For at his best Palés never compromised: structure and discourse operate at the same high level of complexity. Even the supposedly playful Afro-Antillean poems are built on sociolinguistic conventions that are simultaneously subverted. What may have started out as an aesthetic experiment at the expense of black culture ended up transforming his white consciousness and preconceptions—to a qualified degree, if one considers the self-destructive play with racist humor. On the other hand, a clearer consciousness is evoked by the *structure* of his Afro-Antillean poems, which simultaneously celebrate both a non-Western and a Western linguistic consciousness and a fusion of two minds. If one approaches the Afro-Antillean poems without preconceptions of what Caribbean or any other *poesía negra* is supposed to be, Palés celebration of a spiritual and biological *mulatez* was revolutionary.

However belittling of African culture either the popular images or the scientific data of his time may have been, Palés identified a cultural kinship that, radical for his time, inspirited a complete re-evaluation of the *jíbaro* promoted by Puerto Rico's "official" culture. But his writing the poems about that African *numen* in *Tuntún* simultaneously continued a personal process of contemplating, as he had in earlier poetry, the mystery of his inner mental and spiritual self. Sometime between his writing of the Afro-Antillean poems and his oncoming personal maturity, Palés came to realize that, as Heidegger phrased it, poetry was "the foundation which support[ed] history, and therefore . . . not a mere appearance of culture, and absolutely not the mere 'expression' of a 'culture soul'" (Heidegger, 35). In other words, as an aging man and poet in love, the historical and cultural authenticity reached in *Tuntún* was followed by the logical step of his reflecting on his essence, reflections that produced the Filí-Melé cycle.

Thus the "Mulata-Antilla," who in *Tuntún* embodied his cultural numen, was also prefiguring in a narrow "culture soul" context the later Filí-Melé, the existential essence of his poet self, a woman/site/essence with her mulatto hair flowing and yet sprouting fronds and hived by bees. The Filí-Melé cycle, then, proves to be a surprising extension to, not a departure from the Afro-Antillean poems, continuing his expression of the alternate, non-Western epistemology that informed his Afro-Antillean poetry. In this, once again, he either merely coincided with or intentionally emulated Heidegger. James L. Perotti's description of Heidegger's sense of the Logos (Heidegger's version of Filí-Melé) and his attempt to go beyond Western metaphysics fittingly summarizes Palés's pursuit, as if Perotti had been writing about Luis Palés Matos:

These passages in Das Ding can be understood only as mythico-poetic telling and showing of a primitive world. Heidegger makes use of this return to primitive experiences to tell us how, in this case, a thing can be understood as a place where the Logos collects itself instead of being simply a metaphysical res, or object. Thus, this is a return to premetaphysical ways of thinking; this is an attempt to recapture those primordial experiences of the world, the openness of Being that have been almost completely forgotten. . . .

. . . Heidegger's task is to show his contemporaries the advantages of the mythical approach over the literal theological approach. He must point out that sacredness and spirituality have come to be identified with non-physical, non-concrete, the pure, the immaterial, the soulish, the intellectual. He must point out that the divinity of the god is also characterized by those terms. (Perotti, 108–9)

Notes

Chapter 1. *Poetry and Antipoetry: From* Canciones *to* Tuntún

1. Other epithets used are *negrista, negroide, mulata, Afrocubana* and *afroantillana.*

2. (New York: New York University, 1979), 8.

3. Here Grossman was citing from an interview with Antonio Skármeta, 8.

4. Grossman informs us in a footnote that this idea was taken from remarks made by Parra at a poetry reading held at New York University in May, 1970, 9.

5. *Los Poetas Comunicantes* 2d ed. (México: Marcha Editores, 1981), 15. Unless otherwise noted, quotations in English from writings with Spanish-language titles and authors are translations, and all translations of prose and poetry in this book are by Julio Marzán.

6. (Barcelona: Seix Barral, 1981), 13.

7. Ibáñez Langlois, 13.

8. *Sóngoro Cosongo* (Buenos Aires: Editorial Losada, 1967), 47.

9. "La poesía negrista como movimiento literario fue inaugurada hacia 1926 por el puertorriqueño Luis Palés Matos y fue enriquecida por las aportaciones capitales de Nicolás Guillén, Emilio Ballagas, Regino Pedroso, Manuel del Cabral y sus seguidores." Mónica Mansour, *La Poesía Negrista* (Mexico: Ediciones Era, 1973), 9.

10. Luis Palés Matos, *Poesía Completa y Prosa Selecta,* ed. Margot Arce de Vázquez (Caracas: Biblioteca Ayacucho, 1978), 159. All quotations of Palés Matos's poetry are taken from this edition.

11. *Vocabulario Puertorriqueño* (Sharon, Conn.: The Troutman Press, 1965), 54.

12. *Obras de Antonio S. Pedreira* book 1, ed. Concha Meléndez (San Juan: Instituto de Cultura Puertorriqueña, 1970), 37.

13. Bernal Díaz del Canel, "Luis Palés Matos: Intelectual Puertorriqueño," *Los Quijotes* November 17, 1927, 6–8, in Palés, 211.

14. Cited and translated by Grossman, 11, from Leonidas Morales T., *La Poesía de Nicanor Parra* (Santiago de Chile: Universidad Austral de Chile and Editorial Andrés Bellos, 1972), 192.

15. Williams's free verse really encoded a baroque imagination influenced by Góngora. This unorthodox view of Williams's Puerto Rican half and Spanish American roots is the subject of my book *The Spanish American Roots of Williams Carlos Williams* (Austin: University of Texas Press, 1994).

16. This was an evening graduate class held during a spring semester and not the "Summer Seminar" Grossman attended.

17. See José Luis González, *País de los Cuatro Pisos* (Río Piedras: Editorial Huracán, 1980).

18. *Poliedro,* San Juan, December 4, 1926, I, 4, 4–5, in Palés Matos, 207.

19. This split personality prevails to this day, even as Spain has been replaced by the United States as the popular Western model of choice: today's statehood

advocates have only won popularity when they moved closer to promising a "Jíbaro State," one that promises to keep the island's Spanish and its Hispanic character.

20. Angela Negrón Muñoz, "Hablando con Don Luis Palés Matos" *El Mundo*, San Juan, P.R., 13 November 1932, in Palés Matos, 213–24. As a courteous concession to a visiting poet, it would seem, Palés made it a point to add rather rhetorically "and the miracles being performed by González Martín," who had been visiting Puerto Rico. Of González Martín, who had filled up a small auditorium on several nights, Palés noted in a flattering but less assertive tone the Spaniard's "gifts as a reader, . . . the wealth of his repertory in whose depths beats the lively accent of a people. . . ."

21. Enrique Anderson Imbert and Eugenio Florit, *Literatura Hispanoamericana: Antología e Introducción Histórica* (New York: Holt, Rinehart and Winston, 1960), 673.

22. *Luis Palés Matos: un poeta puertorriqueño* (San Juan: Biblioteca de Autores Puertorriqueños, 1937), 23.

Chapter 2. Palés Matos and His Critics

1. *The American Mercury*, XXI, no. 295, 1930, 75.

2. *El Mundo* (San Juan, P.R.), November 1932.

3. Published in *Alma Latina*, San Juan, February 1933. Cited by Federico De Onís in his introduction to *Poesías 1915–1956*, 3d ed. (San Juan: Universidad de Puerto Rico, 1968), 16.

4. Published in Margot Arce de Vázquez, *Impresiones* (San Juan: Yaurel, 1950), 47.

5. Antonio S. Pedreira, *Obras de Antonio S. Pedreira*, book 1 (San Juan: Instituto de Cultura Puertorriqueña, 1970), 66–67.

6. Cited by Federico De Onís in his introduction to Luis Palés Matos, *Poesía 1915–1956* (San Juan: Editorial Universitaria, 1957), 17.

7. "Dedicación al Homenaje," *Asomante*, XV, no. 3 (1959), 7–8.

8. Jean Franco, *The Modern Culture of Latin America* (Middlesex: Penguin Books Ltd., 1967), 133.

9. 18 April–June (1974), pages unnumbered.

10. Manuel Maldonado Denis, *Puerto Rico: Una Interpretación Histórico-Social* (Mexico: Editorial Siglo XXI, 1969), 133.

11. One has to question, however, the lumping of all poetry—by Afro-American poets and merely about Afro-American subjects—in the same category. Would we call a poem by Guillén about Martí "poesía blanquista"? White poets on black themes are also included in José Luis González and Mónica Monsour, *Poesía Negra de América* (México: Ediciones Era, 1976).

12. (Humacao: Editorial Furudí, 1975), II, 126.

13. The term "agapito," according to Arce, refers to Agapito's Bar, apparently a hangout for pro-statehood islanders. See Palés, 183.

14. Arcadio Díaz Quiñones, "La Poesía Negra de Luis Palés Matos: Realidad y Conciencia de Su Dimensión Colectiva." *Sin Nombre*, I, no. 1 (1970), 11.

15. Raúl Hernández Novás, "Introducción" in Luis Palés Matos, *Poesía* (La Habana: Casa de las Américas, n.d.), xxi.

16. Nor did Díaz quote Hernández at any point. Hernández's book gives no year of publication, so we cannot tell which came first.

17. *Impresiones*, 43–51.

18. La Torre, VIII, no. 29–30 (1960), 163–87.

19. José I. De Diego Padró, *Luis Palés Matos y su trasmundo poético* (Río Piedras: Ediciones Puerto, 1973), 30.

20. Quoted in de Diego Padró, 31, from Bernal Díaz de Caney, "Entrevistas confidenciales: Luis Palés Matos, intelectual puertorriqueño," *Los Quijotes*, September 17, 1927, 6–8.27

Chapter 4. The Totemic Word

1. These first three examples, from *Palacio en Sombra*, predate "Orquestación diepálica" and, being only a sampling of the onomatopoetic devices in Palés's early poetry, serve to disprove the claim that the poet's penchant for such devices was the influence of José I. De Diego Padró. Their collaboration was apparently the natural association of like spirits.

2. This parallels Nicolás Guillén's lines in "West Indies Ltd." describing the Caribbean islands as ports that speak an English that begins and ends with the word "yes."

3. Manuel Alvarez Nasario, *El elemento afronegroide en el español de Puerto Rico* (San Juan: Instituto de Cultura Puertorriqueña), 303–404.

Chapter 5. Images of the Numen

1. Federico de Onís placed this poem among Palés's later, post *Tuntún* works; Arce de Vázquez strangely grouped it among the Afro-Antillean poems.

2. The Arce de Vázquez edition has two poems by that title. The one cited here is grouped under "Otros Poemas (1917–1918)," 99. An earlier version "Tic-Tac" and even earlier version of "Voz" is included among the poems of the unpublished book "El Palacio en Sombras (1918–1919)."

Chapter 6. A Grammar of Palés's Style

1. Note that "magazín" is one of several Puerto Rican Anglicisms Palés employs. This is another example of writing "en boricua."

2. See M. Arce de Vázquez's introduction in *Poesía completa*, xvi.

3. Quoted in Mónica Mansour, *La poesía negrista* (México: Ediciones Era, 1973), 159.

4. Artes y Letras, No. 10 (1954), 3–5.

5. Alvarez cites Palés's lines as translations of "Adombe ganga mondé" but neither confirms nor denies their accuracy. The Afro-Cuban singer Celia Cruz, on one of her recordings, "Toro Mata" repeats "mondé" as a refrained exhortation to sustain the tempo of music/dance. This usage should confirm that, indeed, the word conveyed the idea of "bailar" and, by extension, "festejar," so "comer" would not be farfetched.

6. Rubén del Rosario, *Vocabulario Puertorriqueño* (Sharon, Conn.: The Troutman Press, 1965), 103.

7. See Chapter 2, note 13.

Chapter 7. The Numinous Site: The "Filí-Melé" Cycle

1. VIII, no. 29–30 (1960), 9–37.

2. *La Torre*, 21.

3. "Conversación con Juan Antonio Corretjer" in *Ventana*, No. 2, segunda epoca (1976), 8.

4. James L. Perroti, *Heidegger on the Divine: The Thinker, the Poet and God* (Athens: Ohio University Press, 1946), 83.

5. Cited in Perotti, 99.

6. Quoted from "Remembrance of the Poet" in Perotti, 99.

7. Martin Heidegger, "Holderlein and the Essence of Poetry," in *European Literary Theory and Practice: From Existential Phenomenology to Structuralism*, ed. Vernon W. Gras (New York: Dell Publishing Co., 1973), 35.

8. Thomas Langan, *The Meaning of Heidegger: A Critical Study of an Existential Phenomenology* (New York: Columbia University Press, 1966), 199.

9. Luis Palés Matos, *Poesías (1915–1956)* (San Juan: Editorial Universidad de Puerto Rico), 1957.

10. In her Ayacucho edition, Arce arranged the sonnets in this sequence.

Bibliography

Primary Sources

Palés Matos, Luis. *Azaleas*. Introduction by Manuel A. Martínez Dávila. Guayama: Editorial Rodríguez y Cía., 1915.

———. *Poesía completa y prosa selecta*. Edited by Margot Arce de Vázquez. Caracas: Biblioteca Ayacucho, 1978.

———. *Poesía 1915–1956*. Introduced by Federico de Onís. San Juan: Editorial Universitaria, 1971.

———. *Tuntún de pasa y grifería: poemas afro-antillanos*. San Juan: Biblioteca de Autores Puertorriqueños, 1937.

———. *Tuntún de pasa y grifería*. San Juan: Biblioteca de Autores Puertorriqueños, 1950.

———. "Suderman: el camino de los gatos." *Juan Bobo*. San Juan (1917), n.p.

———. "El traje de Medea." *Los Quijotes* (San Juan), II, no. 40 (1926): 3.

Secondary Sources

Agrait, Gustavo. *Luis Palés Matos: un poeta puertorriqueño*. San Juan: Biblioteca de Autores Puertorriqueños, 1973.

———. "Antilla, mujer y amor en la poesía de Luis Palés Matos." *Río Piedras* I, no. 2 (1973): 41–69.

Aleixandre, Vicente. "Encuentro con Luis Palés Matos." *La Torre* VIII, nos. 29–30 (1960), 147–50.

Alonso, Amado. *El problema de la lengua en América*. Madrid: Espasa-Calpe, 1945.

Alvarez Nazario, Manuel. *El elemento afronegroide en el español de Puerto Rico: Contribución al estudio del negro en América*. San Juan: Instituto de Cultura Puertorriqueña, 1974.

———. *La herencia lingüística de Canarias de Puerto Rico*. San Juan: Instituto de Cultura Puertorriqueña, 1972.

Anderson Imbert, E. "Luis Palés Matos: desde la Argentina." *Asomante* XV, no. 3 (1959), 39–40.

Arce de Vázquez, Margot. "Guayama en la poesía de Luis Palés Matos." *Revista del Instituto de Cultura Puertorriqueña* II, no. 3 (1959), 36–38.

———. *Impresiones*. San Juan: Editorial Yaurel, 1950.

———. "Luis Palés Matos, poeta." *Guajana* I, no. 1 (1962) n.p.

———. "El llamado de Luis Palés Matos." *Extramuros* I, no. 2 (1972) 1–11.

———. "Más sobre los poemas negros de Luis Palés Matos." *Ateneo Puertorriqueño*, II (1936), 34–45.

191

————. "Notas para la composición de *Tuntún de pasa y grifería*." Universidad, 30 de septiembre de 1954, n.p.

————. "La poesía negra de Guillén y Palés: coincidencias y discrepancias." *Mairena* Año 1, no. 1 (1979), n.p.

————. "'Puerta al tiempo en tres voces' de Luis Palés Matos." Río Piedras, I, no. 1, (1972), 9–30.

————. "Tres pueblos negros: algunas observaciones sobre el estilo de Luis Palés Matos." *La Torre* VIII, no. 29–30 (1960), 163–87.

————. "Unidad de la obra poética de Luis Palés Matos." *Asomante* XV, no. 3 (1959), 32–38.

Arrigoitia, Luis de. "Anotaciones métricas a la poesía de Luis Palés Matos." *Asomante* XXV, no. 4 (1960), 71–84.

————. "Cuatro poetas puertorriqueños: José de Diego, Luis Lloréns Torres, Luis Palés Matos, Juan Antonio Corretjer." *Caravelle* no. 18 (1972), 9–76.

Astol, Eugenio. "Prólogo a 'El palacio en sombras'." *Puerto Rico Ilustrado* San Juan, XIII, no. 673 (1923), 59–76.

Babín, María Teresa. *Jornadas Literarias*. (Puerto Rico), 1967, 79–80.

Barrera, Héctor. "Renovación poética de Luis Palés Matos." *Asomante* VII, no. 2 (1951), 57–67.

Bayón, Damián Carlos. "Luis Palés Matos, o la creación de un mundo a partir de la poesía." *La Torre* VIII, nos. 29–30, 105–127.

Bedrinana, Francisco C. "La luna en la poesía negra." *Revista* Bimestre Cubana, XXXVII (1936), 12–16.

Bellini, Giuseppe. "Luis Palés Matos, intérprete del alma antillana." *Asomante* XV, no. 3 (1959), 20–31.

Benedetti, Mario. *Los poetas comunicantes* 2d ed. Mexico: Marcha Editores, 1981.

Benítez, Jaime. "Homenaje a Palés: introducción." *La Torre* VIII, nos. 29–30 (1960), 9–37.

————. "Luis Palés Matos y el pesimismo en Puerto Rico." Introduction to *Tuntún de pasa y grifería*. San Juan: Biblioteca de Autores Puertorriqueños, 1950, 9–37.

Blanco, Angel. "Poesía y revolución: sobre Luis Palés Matos." *Claridad* 28 de febrero de 1971, 22.

Blanco, Tomás. "A Puerto Rican poet: Luis Palés Matos." *The American Mercury* XXI, no. 81 (1930), 2–75.

————. *Sobre Palés*. San Juan: Biblioteca de Autores Puertorriqueños, 1920.

————. "Dos preguntas sobre la poesía de Palés Matos." Caribe, I, no. 2 (1941), 20–21.

————. "En familia: sobre L. Palés Matos." El Mundo, 19 de febrero de 1933.

————. "Escorzos de un poeta antillano: Luis Palés Matos." *Revista Bimestre Cubana* XLII (1938), 221–40.

————. "Margot Arce: Conferencia sobre los poemas negros de Palés." *Ateneo Puertorriqueño*, III (1935), 24–30.

————. "Reincidencia y ratificación: Poesía (1915–1956)." *Revista del Instituto de Cultura Puertorriqueña* I, no. 1 (1958), 35–37.

Braschi, Wilfredo. "Nuevas tendencias en la literatura puertorriqueña." In *Li-*

teratura puertorriqueña: 21 conferencias. San Juan: Instituto de Cultura Puertorriqueña, 1969, 539–52.

Cabrera, Francisco Manrique. *Historia de la literature puertorriqueña.* New York: Las Américas Publishing Co., 1956.

Canino Salgado, Marcelino. "Tres versiones del poema 'San Sabas' de Luis Palés Matos." *Mairena* Año 1, no. 1 (1979), n.p.

Corretjer, Juan Antonio. "Lo que no fue Palés." *Revista del Instituto de la Cultura Puertorriqueña* II, no. 3 (1959), p. 35.

Cumpiano, Elisa I. "El paisaje interior en la poesía de Luis Palés Matos." *Mairena* Año 1, no. 1 (1979), n.p.

Curet de Anda, Mirian. "Zoología en Palés." *Revista de Estudios Hispánicos* II, nos. 1–4 (1952), 191–222.

Díaz Quiñonez, Arcadio. "Notas para el estudio del *Tuntún de pasa y grifería. Insula* 4 (1976), 356–57.

––––––. "El Palés de Consuelo Gotay." *Sin Nombre* IV, no. 6 (1976), 82–87.

––––––. "La poesía negra de Luis Palés Matos: realidad y conciencia de su dimensión colectiva." *Sin Nombre* I, no. 1 (1970), 7–25.

Diego, Gerardo. "La palabra poética de Luis Palés Matos." *La Torre* VIII, nos. 29–30 (1960), 29–30.

Diego Padró De, José I. Luis Palés Matos y su trasmundo poético. *Río Piedras:* Ediciones Puerto, 1973.

Enguídanos, Miguel. *La poesía de Luis Palés Matos.* Río Piedras: Editorial Universitaria, 1961.

––––––. "Lo que Palés añadió a Puerto Rico." *La Torre* VIII, nos. 29–30 (1960), 49–65.

Florit, Eugenio. "El mar en los versos de Palés Matos." *Asomante* XV, no. 3 (1959), 7–62.

Font Saldaña, Jorge. "El negro lírico de Luis Palés Matos." *Puerto Rico Ilustrado* XXVII, no. 1474 (1938), p.22, 8–59.

Gallego Larrea, Cristóbal. "Mapa de la poesía afroantillana." *Revista de América* XXII (1950), 173–87.

Géigel Polanco, Vicente. "Los ismos en la década de los veinte." *Literatura puertorriqueña: 21 conferencias.* San Juan: Insituto de Cultura Puertorriqueña, 1969, 263–90.

González, José Emilio. "La individualidad poética de Luis Palés Matos." *La Torre* VIII, nos. 29–30 (1960), 291–329.

––––––. "Luis Palés Matos." In *La poesía contemporánea de Puerto Rico (1930–1960).* San Juan: Instituto de Cultura Puertorriqueña, 1972.

––––––. "Tres danzas negras de Luis Palés Matos." *Asomante* XXV, no. 4 (1969), 20–33.

––––––. "Los poetas puertorriqueños en la década de 1930." *Literatura puertorriqueña: 21 conferencias.* San Juan: Insituto de Cultura Puertorriqueña, 1969, 291–318.

Gullón, Ricardo. "Situación de Palés Matos." *La Torre,* VIII, nos. 29–30 (1960), 35–43.

Hadlich, Roger L. *A Transformational Grammar of Spanish.* Englewood Cliffs, N.J.: Prentice-Hall, 1971.

Heidegger, Martin. "Hölderlein and the Essence of Poetry." *European Literary Theory and Practice: From Existential Phenomenology to Structuralism.* Edited by Vernon W. Gras. New York: Dell Publishing Co., 1973.

Henríquez Ureña, Max. "Recuerdos y apreciaciones en torno a Luis Palés Matos." *La Torre* VIII, nos. 29–30 (1960), 129–43.

Kany, Charles E. *Semántica hispanoamericana.* Translated by Luis Escolar Bareño. Madrid: Aguilar, 1969.

Lavandero, Ramón. "Luis Palés Matos y el negrismo poético antillano." *Ateneo Puertorriqueño* II, (1936), 48–50.

Lloréns, Wáshington. "La jitanjáfora en Luis Palés Matos." *Artes y Letras* no. 10 (1954), 3–5.

Maldonado-Denis, Manuel. *Puerto Rico: Una Interpretación Histórico-Social.* México: Siglo Veintiuno Editores, 1969.

Llora Mora, Francisco. "Cuatro estudios del sentimiento religioso en la poesía de Palés Matos." *El Mundo* 26 de agosto de 1961, 25.

Matos Paoli, Francisco. *Diario de un poeta.* Río Piedras: Ediciones Puerto, 1973.

――――. "El paisaje en la poesía de Luis Palés Matos." *Alma Latina* XV (1945), 31.

Meléndez, Concha. "Presencia jesucristiana en la poesía de Luis Palés Matos." *Asomante* XXV, no. 3 (1950), 63–66.

Morales, Angel Luis. "Julio Herrara y Reissig y Luis Palés Matos: notas sobre un influjo." *Asomante* XXV, no. 4 (1969), 34–53.

――――. "Puerta al tiempo en tres voces." *Mairena* Año 1, no. 1 (1979), n.p.

Morales Oliver, Luis. "Dos aspectos en la poesía de Palés Matos." *Revista del Instituto de Cultura Puertorriqueña* IX, no. 33 (1966), 11–17.

Navarro, Tomás. *El español en Puerto Rico.* Río Piedras: Editorial Universitaria, 1974.

Onís, Federico de. *Luis Palés Matos (1898–1959): vida y obra.* San Juan: Ediciones Ateneo Puertorriqueño, 1960.

――――. "Programa silvestre: Reconstrucción de un tema de Luis Palés." *La Torre* VIII, nos. 29–30 (1960), 189–202.

Pérez-Marchand, Monalisa. "Luis Palés Matos, una conciencia lúcida." *Asomante* XXV, no. 4 (1969), 55–70.

Perroti, James L. *Heidegger on the Divine: The Thinker, the Poet and God.* Athens: Ohio University Press, 1946.

Polit, Carlos E. "Imagen inocente del negro en cuatro poetas antillanos." *Sin Nombre* 5, II (1974) 43–60.

Pozo, Ivania Del. "Language and Silence in Contemporary Spanish-American Literature: As Treated by the Puerto Rican Poet Luis Palés Matos." *Centerpoint* I, No. 1 (1974), 85–89.

Puebla, Manuel de la. "Notas en torno a la bibliografía sobre Palés." *Mairena,* Año 1, no. 1 (1979), n.p.

Ramos Mimosa, Adriana. "El modernismo en la lírica puertorriqueña." *Literatura puertorriqueña: 21 conferencias.* San Juan: Insituto de Cultura Puertorriqueña, 1969, 179–208.

Rivera de Alvarez, Josefina. Diccionario de la literatura puertorriqueña, 2 tomos, 4 vols. Río Piedras: Ediciones de la Torre, 1955.

――――. "Visión histórico-crítica de la literatura puertorriqueña." *Literatura puer-*

torriqueña: 21 conferencias. San Juan: Insituto de Cultura Puertorriqueña, 1969, 33–64.

Rojas, Víctor J. "Sobre el negro en la poesía de Luis Palés Matos y de Jorge Lima." *Sin Nombre* II, no. 3 (1972), 75–88.

Russell, Dora Isella. "Isla, trópico negro y universo en la poesía de Luis Palés Matos." *Revista del Instituto de la Cultura Puertorriqueña* VI, no. 20 (1963), 7–10.

Torre, Guillermo de. "La poesía negra de Luis Palés Matos." *La Torre* VIII, nos. 29–30 (1960), 151–61.

Torres, Lucy. "The Black Poetry of Luis Palés Matos." Diss., Indiana University, 1970.

Valbuena Prat, Angel. "Sobre la poesía de Luis Palés Matos y los temas negros." Introduction to *Tuntún de pasa y grifería: poemas afro-antillanos.* San Juan: Biblioteca de Autores Puertorriqueños, 1937, 9–21.

Index

197